Jack the Ripper - The Policeman

Jack the Ripper - The Policeman

The Complete History of the Jack the Ripper Murders

ROD BEATTIE

First published in Great Britain in 2022 by
Pen & Sword True Crime
An imprint of
Pen & Sword Books Ltd
Yorkshire – Philadelphia

Copyright © Rod Beattie 2022

ISBN 978 1 39901 752 7

The right of Rod Beattie to be identified as Author of this work has been asserted by him in accordance with the Copyright, Designs and Patents Act 1988.

A CIP catalogue record for this book is available from the British Library.

All rights reserved. No part of this book may be reproduced or transmitted in any form or by any means, electronic or mechanical including photocopying, recording or by any information storage and retrieval system, without permission from the Publisher in writing.

Printed and bound in the UK by CPI Group (UK) Ltd, Croydon, CR0 4YY.

Pen & Sword Books Limited incorporates the imprints of Atlas, Archaeology, Aviation, Discovery, Family History, Fiction, History, Maritime, Military, Military Classics, Politics, Select, Transport, True Crime, Air World, Frontline Publishing, Leo Cooper, Remember When, Seaforth Publishing, The Praetorian Press, Wharncliffe Local History, Wharncliffe Transport, Wharncliffe True Crime and White Owl.

For a complete list of Pen & Sword titles please contact

PEN & SWORD BOOKS LIMITED
47 Church Street, Barnsley, South Yorkshire, S70 2AS, England
E-mail: enquiries@pen-and-sword.co.uk
Website: www.pen-and-sword.co.uk

Or

PEN AND SWORD BOOKS
1950 Lawrence Rd, Havertown, PA 19083, USA
E-mail: Uspen-and-sword@casematepublishers.com
Website: www.penandswordbooks.com

Contents

Acknowledgements   vii

Chapter 1   A Disgruntled Officer   1

Chapter 2   The Cass Case   13

Chapter 3   Back in the Dock   31

Chapter 4   Martha Tabram – Murdered 7 August 1888   45

Chapter 5   Mary Ann Nichols – Murdered 31 August 1888   49

Chapter 6   The Search for the Ripper   61

Chapter 7   Annie Chapman – Murdered 8 September 1888   67

Chapter 8   Elizabeth Stride – Murdered 30 September 1888   79

Chapter 9   Catherine Eddowes – Murdered 30 September 1888   91

Chapter 10   Mary Jane Kelly – Murdered 9 November 1888   105

Chapter 11   The Other Victims   119

Bibliography   127

Index   129

Acknowledgements

Special thanks go to my publishers, Pen and Sword Books, especially Jonathan Wright, who first offered to publish it, and Kate Bohdanowicz, who did an outstanding job of editing it. Thank you to all of you who helped.

I would also like to thank my wonderful partner Breda for all her help and encouragement when things were difficult and I wanted just to forget about it. Thank you for keeping me going and for the tea.

Also, my lovely daughter Emma for continually asking, 'How's the book going?' It's finished and no you can't sell a signed copy!

Special thanks must also go to Aine Keohane, a very talented young graphic artist who created a wonderful design for the cover. I know she will go far in her chosen profession.

Thanks must also go to the staff at the National Archives in Kew for all their help and the Devon and Metropolitan Police archivists who searched for the information I needed.

Thank you for reading the book and I hope you enjoy it.

CHAPTER 1

A Disgruntled Officer

In a survey run by a national newspaper, it was revealed that readers consider Jack the Ripper to be the most evil Briton of the last 1,000 years. The only reason for this, I believe, is that the identity of Jack was never revealed. This makes him someone to be frightened of, a man who can kill at will and never be captured – the antithesis of everything wholesome that normal people believe in.

Could it be that the identity of Jack was known but withheld for the well-being of the country? If it were acknowledged that the man who became known as Jack the Ripper had at one time been partially responsible for riots taking place in London, and had nearly brought down the government, there would have been absolute chaos, especially when it was revealed that Jack was in fact a policeman.

When I began to do research for this book I thought, as many of my contemporaries have done in their own books, that my suspect could have been the real murderer. It was only after many visits and countless hours wading through the files at the Public Records Office in Kew, and trips to Devon where my suspect was born, that I began to get a picture of exactly who he was and what he was like, and the more I delved into the records of the Metropolitan Police, the more convinced I became that at last the truth about the murders – and who committed them – had been found.

With the amount of police officers that had been drafted in to patrol the East End of London as the murders progressed, no one could have continually got away with the attacks unless that person was involved with the police. A police officer is the only person who could have walked the streets at night knowing that he would not be questioned or suspected of being the killer.

It is my belief that he continued to murder up until at least 1892, but changed his *modus operandi* because he knew that the police suspected him. But even knowing the risk he was taking he was still unable to control his thirst for revenge (more of why I believe this was revenge later).

It is impossible to believe that during the later murders by Jack the Ripper, when the whole area was on alert, anyone who was not in hiding in plain sight – as an officer of the law – could have walked around the streets at night, committed the murders and

Bowden Endacott photographed upon his retirement. (*Courtesy of the Metropolitan Police*)

just walked away again. There were far too many police officers patrolling the area, and as the prostitutes knew that any of them could be the next victim they were wary of all strangers. There have been countless theories as to who the murderer was, but if you look at the murders logically, only one type of person could have committed them all and got away with it. As Sir Arthur Conan Doyle said, 'when you have eliminated the impossible, whatever remains, *however improbable*, must be the truth.'

The 'improbable' fact that we have to look at is that the only person who would not have been suspected and who had a reason for being on the streets is a police officer. Someone whom the prostitutes knew and believed they could trust. Eddowes, the fourth victim of the so-called canonical five (Mary Ann Nichols, Annie Chapman, Elizabeth Stride, Catherine Eddowes and Mary Jane Kelly), stated that she had come back to London to earn the reward offered for the capture of the killer as she thought she knew him. She was later seen by three witnesses talking to the killer in a friendly way. No prostitute would have taken that chance unless it was someone she knew well and believed that, because of his position in society, she could trust him. Mary Jane Kelly, who was murdered in her home, would not have taken a man to her room unless she was sure she could trust him. It has to have been someone the prostitutes knew well and the only person this fits is a man who, as a police officer whose job it was to keep them off the streets, they knew extremely well.

Although we can look at old photographs and read old reports and documents, it is difficult for us to comprehend in these days of plenty the complete and utter poverty and deprivation people in the East End of London were forced to live in during the latter part of the nineteenth century. Crime, violence, immorality, and drunkenness were the normal way of life for most of the people who lived there.

Many of the streets were small and dingy, with back-to-back housing. In 1893, Thomas Henry Huxley gave a lecture at Oxford entitled, 'Evolution and Ethics', and said of the area: 'I have seen the Polynesian savaging and in his primitive condition, before the missionary or the blackbirder or the beachcomber got at him. With all his savaging, he was not half so savage, so unclean, so irreclaimable, as the tenant of a tenement in an East End slum.' It was estimated that of a total population of 47,000 living in the Whitechapel area, 23,000 – almost half – were living in poverty. By poverty, it meant those people faced starvation on a daily basis, and had no way of earning money to feed themselves or their families.

The area was nothing more than a network of narrow streets, courts, and alleyways, with offshoots often ending in rookeries: it has been compared to a rabbit warren. Gangs terrorised different areas, taking protection money, primarily from the prostitutes, or 'unfortunates', as they were known. The cry of 'Murder!' was so common at night that invariably it was ignored.

The members of the community who were lucky enough to find employment either worked in one of the local markets – such as Spitalfields Market – or at London Docks. There was high unemployment and in 1888 it was estimated that 20-25,000 men were out of work in the East End, the majority of them their family's sole breadwinner. Wages were also low and this made for a largely transient population – those that did stay lived in one of the many tenements or common lodging houses that saturated the area. In many parts of the East End, particularly around the back streets off the Whitechapel Road, some houses similar in aspect to those a century or more ago can still be seen. To give some idea of what it must have been like, we only have to look at a letter from Sir James Frazer, commissioner of the City of London Police, to Godfrey Lushington, the permanent under-secretary of state, in which it was stated that the area in Whitechapel covered by Metropolitan Police's H Division, had 233 common lodging houses, sixty-two brothels and 1,200 prostitutes. It was an area that Victorian writer Jack London called 'the abyss'.

H Division required heavy policing and officers usually made their rounds in pairs. Some parts of the district were no-go areas where the police never entered, and the Whitechapel police met with so much habitual crime and street deaths that by the 1880s, inquest juries were very reticent about describing bodies found as murder victims unless they showed obvious signs of having been murdered.

The Ripper murders caused a wave of horror that pervaded all aspects of the normally staid society of Victorian England. Questions were asked in Parliament, and even Queen Victoria sent a telegram to Prime Minister Lord Salisbury, insisting that the new detective service must improve and that the courts and alleyways in Whitechapel, where the murders had occurred, must be better lit. Three days later, on 13 November 1888, she sent a letter to Home Secretary Henry Matthews, stating that she thought the detective force was inefficient, and offered her own suggestions of what steps the police should take in order to find the murderer.

At the time of the Whitechapel murders, much infighting and squabbling was taking place between the police and the Home Office. Many observers at the time believed that there would have been a better chance of solving the mystery had the assistant metropolitan commissioner in charge of CID – James Monro – been left to do police work with no interference from the Home Office. Monro was liked and admired by practically everyone who worked with him – he fought for pension rights for the ordinary policeman on the beat, and this endeared him to them. Apart from the Home Office, the only other senior police officer who disagreed with Monro's methods and attitudes was his immediate superior, Sir Charles Warren, the Metropolitan Police commissioner. Warren's background was in the military service and on appointment to the post, he assumed he would rule the force with military discipline. Monro, on the other hand, knew that this was not the way for the police force to be accepted by the public, nor by the ordinary policeman, who, in the majority of cases, was an ordinary person with no military experience.

Monro had also been given his own secret department, operating separately from CID and the uniformed branch. This department, known officially as 'Section D' and unofficially as 'Special Branch' had been set up to observe anarchists and subversives, and also immigrants who might use asylum in London to plot terrorism. This gave Monro direct access to the Home Secretary and Warren resented this; his military career having given him the notion that as commissioner he and he alone should have access to the upper echelon of the land. The Home Secretary, however, was quite happy with the situation and this caused the relationship between him and Warren to become even more strained. It should be noted here that the opinion at the time was that Matthews, whilst being an exceedingly able lawyer, was quite incapable of dealing with men.

The majority of the radical press disliked Warren, and *The Star* newspaper demanded his resignation as the Whitechapel murders developed, with the conservative press ultimately following suit. Warren was accused of introducing mindless militarism into the police force, of demoralising the CID, and of following Matthews' frivolous do-nothing lead. He was mocked for letting bloodhounds try to track him through Regents Park, but then decided they would not be able to track through the crowded city streets in order to locate the Ripper. It was claimed that one of the two dogs – Burgho and Barnaby – who had been offered to Warren by a Mr Edwin Brough, who was keen to do his bit to get the Ripper off the streets, bit Warren at the trials, but this has proved to be an invention of the press in order for them to make Warren appear as comical as they believed he was. Warren responded to press attacks on him by publishing an article in *Murray's Magazine* entitled 'The Police of the Metropolis'. This was against approved procedure and Warren must have been aware that officials were expected to seek clearance from Home Office senior civil servants before submitting articles for publication. He could not have relished the idea though of asking for approval from men with whom he had such a bad relationship.

The Home Secretary responded to Warren's article by issuing a memorandum inviting his immediate resignation. Warren offered it in response, stating that had he realised the rule regarding the publication of articles also applied to him, he would never have taken up the post as commissioner. His resignation was announced on 9 November 1888, ironically only a few weeks after that of Monro who had resigned in October. The details of Warren's resignation were released on the day that the mutilated body of Mary Jane Kelly was found. It was claimed that the murder had forced his resignation but the fact is that it was the climax of a struggle that had been going on between the Home Office and the Metropolitan Police for fifty years. It was only a coincidence that his resignation occurred on the day of the murder, his resignation letter having been sent a few days earlier. Cynics have suggested his departure was deliberately announced a few hours after the murder in order for the Home Office to be able to show that they were in fact doing something about the murders.

Through all of this infighting, the work of the police on the front line had to continue. H Division station was, and still is, situated about half way down Leman Street. Adjoining it at the time was the

Garrick Theatre, which later moved to the Charing Cross Road. It was between the officers stationed in Leman Street that questions about the similarity of the murders first began to be asked.

The body of Mary Ann, or 'Polly' Nichols, a prostitute, had been found on 31 August 1888 in Buck's Row in Whitechapel. She had been murdered, and her body had been mutilated. A similar murder had taken place two weeks earlier, that of Martha Tabram, also a prostitute. Her body had been found in George Yard, Whitechapel on 7 August. Although Martha's injuries were not exactly the same as those of Polly Nichols, the severity of the attacks made the police believe that they were connected. The officers feared that a maniac was possibly on the loose, and those fears were founded when another body was discovered on 8 September. The victim, another prostitute, was Annie Chapman. The police noted that the body, found in a back yard in Hanbury Street, again in Whitechapel, had also been mutilated; this time a lot more severely than the previous victims.

The night of 30 September came and with it not one but two murders, again two prostitutes, Elizabeth Stride and Catherine Eddowes, and again with similar mutilations. Then a month went by with no more murders. Suddenly, on the morning of Friday 9 November, the murderer struck again. The victim was Mary Jane Kelly and her body was found in Miller's Court, Dorset Street. She was the only one of the victims to have been murdered indoors and the assailant virtually tore her body apart. She was the youngest of the victims and most people now believe that she was the last of the victims of the man who became known as Jack the Ripper.

★ ★ ★

In 1988, a number of psychological profiles were drawn up to commemorate the 100th anniversary of the worldwide phenomenon of Britain's most infamous serial killer.

An analysis of the Ripper's background, behaviour and *modus operandi* was made at the pioneering Behavioural Science Unit of the FBI academy in Quantico, Virginia, and the files were studied in an attempt to understand his personality and build up his history. It was surmised that the killer was raised in a family with a domineering mother, and a weak or absent father. The boy would have grown up without the constant care and attention of a stable, adult role model. He would have had a diminished emotional response towards people in general and his anger would gradually have been felt when he realised exactly what his family life was like. This anger would have been internalised, and he would have probably developed a fantasy life in order to compensate for it. This fantasy life would have probably included the domination of women.

As an adult, his colleagues would have seen him as a loner and he would have been noted as being quiet, shy, and obedient, but with an inner rebellious streak that sometimes made him resist authority. His dress would have been neat and orderly and he would have looked for employment in a position where he could work alone so that he could control his surroundings. He would not have been proficient at meeting other people and would have preferred his own company.

The murderer must have had a disciplined mind in order not to leave any clues or weapons at the scene of his crimes, and to avoid the many police patrols. As a strict and regimented murderer, he would have been intelligent and articulate, would have probably lived with a female partner, and would have held a steady, skilled job. The disciplined murderer often kills when situational stress compels him to do so. With the disorganised offender, no external trigger is needed – just a deep rage and hostility lying within his personality. He would have been disorganised in that he did not plan his crimes, apart from possibly Catherine Eddowes in Mitre Square (of which more later), or stalk his victims, and he left the bodies unhidden.

It is likely that Jack the Ripper fitted the FBI's bill to a tee. To the outside world, he would have been seen as a normal happily married man with a good job. Internally, he would have been raging at injustices he felt had been done to him, and his anger would have been vented in the only way possible to sate his lust for revenge, by murdering those he thought had wronged him.

In a report he prepared for Dr Robert Anderson, assistant commissioner of the Metropolitan Police, following the murder of Mary Jane Kelly in Dorset Street, Dr Thomas Bond made the following observations:

> He must in my opinion be a man subject to periodical attacks of Homicidal and erotic mania. The character of the mutilations indicate that the man may be in a condition sexually, that may be called satyriasis. It is of course possible that the Homicidal impulse may have developed from a revengeful or brooding condition of the mind, or that Religious Mania may have been the original disease, but I do not think either hypothesis is likely.

Although Bond did not believe that revenge was the motive, we now know that this usually plays a great part in a serial killer's profile. We can also assume that the murderer was suffering from paranoia, giving him an acute persecution mania, and it should be noted that paranoia usually reaches a dangerous stage in people who are in their mid-thirties.

The person I propose fitted all of these traits was named Bowden Endacott, and the reason he found it very easy to sate his revengeful lust was because he knew every single aspect of the police enquiries that were being made. He knew where the police officers would have been patrolling, and probably knew most of them by name. The reason for this was that he himself was a police officer.

After more than three years of research into Bowden Endacott and his family, I am convinced that this man is the murderer the world has come to know as Jack the Ripper. Everything fits the description proffered by the FBI: his early life, his attitude towards prostitutes, and the way he must have felt after what happened to him all add up to a man who must have wanted revenge.

Bowden was born on 13 July 1851, in Chagford, a small farming community in Devon. His father, William, was a tailor by trade although most of Bowden's brothers, as well as himself, became farm labourers. It is possible to assume that Bowden had little or no schooling, as on the 1861 census form he is described as nine years old and an agricultural labourer. His mother also appears not to have been literate, as on his birth certificate she signs her name with a cross.

Bowden was the youngest of seven children, six boys and one girl. One of his brothers died in childhood before Bowden was born. This left William, Henry, Ann, John and James, and in 1851, Bowden.

It is believed that Bowden's mother, Elizabeth, ruled her family with a rod of iron. She had come from a strong farming family, and when she married William Endacott, a tailor, on 29 May 1831, she must have believed that she was bettering herself. But this was not the case as William was ineffectual and Elizabeth took over the running of the household, and the upbringing of the children. She cannot have been very pleased when, at the age of 41, she found herself pregnant again, this time with Bowden. It is almost certain he was resented by his strong, domineering mother, and undoubtedly was picked on and shunned by her, thus growing up without the motherly love that every child needs to develop into a normal, stable adult. It would also appear that Bowden was treated like a slave to the household.

Elizabeth lived for another eighteen years after Bowden was born, dying on 5 April 1870, aged 58. Bowden was now left with just his father, his elder brother James, who at 22 was a mason, and a retired farmer named Richard Underhill, who was a lodger – the rest of the family having left home.

Bowden was still a labourer and must have decided that enough was enough now that his mother had died. He applied to join the Devon Constabulary and was accepted by them on 24 May 1872. On his application form it was stated that he was 20 years and 10 months old, single, 5ft 9ins tall with hazel eyes, brown hair, and a pale complexion. On the form Bowden stated that he was a farmer, not, as was the general practice – and the truth in Bowden's case – a farm labourer. His pale complexion also falsified his statement that he was a farmer. This lie, although not serious, shows us that Bowden may have been ashamed of being only a farm labourer and wanted to better himself. It also shows that there could have been internal anger building up in him, due to his deprived family circumstances, his manual job and the fantasy life he wished he led, coming to the fore. Although the police must surely have realised that Bowden was lying, he was accepted into the ranks joining as Third Class Constable 319. It should be noted here that Bowden would lie again later on in his career, but this time in a far more serious situation.

Bowden was stationed at Staverton, and he stayed with the Devon Police for two years and eleven months. Most of his duty was mundane and passed without comment but there were two incidents which undoubtedly affected his future life. The first of these was when a young woman named Miss Rogers, in whose brother's house he lodged, served him with a bastardy order. Miss Rogers also lived in the house, being employed as housekeeper by her brother. Later, at a crucial turning point in his life, Bowden would stoutly deny that it was anything to do with him. However, when he was brought face to face with names, dates and faces, he admitted that it was true, declaring 'that he had settled it, and that he had never seen the woman since, and had never seen the child at all.' At the later inquiry into the Cass case (of which more later), it was suggested that Bowden had left the Devon police force without giving notice because of the incident with Miss Rogers. He strongly denied this saying that he 'gave a month's notice after receiving the affiliation summons, which was served upon him five or six months before the child was born.'

Bowden was also involved in another incident in Witheridge, in Devon. Unfortunately, records of this event have failed to survive the passage of time, but we can assume that it was a serious allegation made against him. Later on, when questioned about this incident, Bowden said 'he had a cousin there, a policeman, of the same name as himself'.

This was an out and out lie; there was never another policeman in the Devon Constabulary named Bowden Endacott. This continual lying gives us another link in the case for Bowden Endacott being Jack the Ripper, as many serial killers are compulsive liars.

His service with the Devon Constabulary was terminated on 8 April 1875, when Bowden resigned from the force. He stated that it was because he 'made application'. What he meant by this we can only assume, but his service parchment that he was given upon leaving speaks for itself. His conduct was described as 'generally good' and his abilities are given as 'moderate'. These two mediocre descriptions were unusual and a damming indictment of his conduct and general attitude, as at this time most third class constables were promoted within twelve to eighteen months to second class. Bowden wasn't. Generally, it would appear that the Devon Constabulary was gratified to see the back of him.

It is not known what Bowden did for the next four months, but by August 1875 he had moved to London, and on 23 August he joined the Metropolitan Police. His warrant number was 59281, and his divisional number was PC115E. E Division covered the Holborn area of London.

It is noteworthy that these warrant numbers are unique to that force and mean nothing to other forces. I am grateful to ex-Metropolitan Police Officer Brian T. Estill (Warrant No. 156892), who is the curator of the Museum of Policing in Devon & Cornwall in Exeter for this piece of information and for the material on Bowden's career in the Devon Police.

By 1877 Bowden was living at 1 Wilson Street in London. On 1 January of that year he married a woman called Emily Caroline Morris, who came from Cheltenham in Gloucestershire and was now living at 6 Wilson Street. By the time of the census register in 1881, it states that they were living at 21 Gower Street and had a son, Bowden Morris, who was three years old.

When Bowden retired in 1900, still a constable, the *Police Review and Parade Gossip* made the following observations:

> Mr Bowden Endacott, who has recently retired from the Metropolitan Police Force, after 25 years' service, performed his first Police duties in the ranks of the Devon Constabulary, in which he served for four years – from 1871 to 1875. In the latter year he joined the Metropolitan Force, and was drafted to the E Division – to the Reserve of which he was appointed as early as 1880 – after a shorter term of probation than is usual. For the last 12 years he has been engaged on special duty at the British Museum.

In the earlier stages of his career in the Metropolitan Force, whilst engaged on street duty, he was connected with the capture of several notorious burglars and the perpetrators of highway robberies with violence, and he has on several occasions received the commendations of Her Majesty's Judges and Grand Juries. He has also been rewarded by the Commissioner for saving life at the risk of his own, on one occasion incurring severe personal injury to himself.

In his capacity of a Constable Mr Endacott endeavoured to exercise what influence he could in regard to the purity and morality of the streets, and it was his zeal in this direction that bought him in 1887 into unusual prominence. This was in connection with what was known as the 'Cass' case.

This Cass case was, I believe, the turning point in Bowden's life. The events that happened finally broke Bowden Endacott, and the inner rage that had for so long been burning inside of him erupted to the surface in a frenzy of murderous revenge.

CHAPTER 2

The Cass Case

At the time of the Cass case in 1887, the relationship between the police and the public was in a precarious position, to say the least. The police were disliked and mistrusted by the populace, and this was in part due to years of bad leadership within the force. Earlier that year, Metropolitan Police Commissioner Sir Charles Warren, who had only been in the job for a little over a year, prohibited the use of Trafalgar Square for large meetings. On 13 November, a meeting was scheduled to be held there in defiance of his orders and a huge crowd gathered. Warren responded by sending in the police to clear them. A bitter conflict arose and eventually the foot guards and the mounted life guards were called in to help. This resulted in two people losing their lives and 100 casualties. The day became known as 'Bloody Sunday', and Warren became reviled amongst the working classes.

Previously to this, on Monday, 8 February 1886, the London Working Men's Committee had gathered in Trafalgar Square to protest about unemployment. They sent a message to Metropolitan Police Commissioner Sir Edmund Yeomans Walcott Henderson, stating that they believed a rival group called the Social Democratic Federation might cause trouble. Henderson did not take the warning seriously and sent only a small company of police reserves, under the command of 74-year-old Divisional Superintendent Robert Walker and, due to a mix up, they were ordered to protect Marlborough House and Buckingham Palace, which kept them away from Trafalgar Square. The heated meeting in the square developed into a riot and the protesters, completely ignoring Marlborough House and Buckingham Palace, marched through the West End of London breaking windows and looting shops.

At D Division's Marylebone Lane Police Station, Inspector Cuthbert was parading his evening relief of one sergeant and fifteen constables when he heard that the rioters were heading his way. Then, in an act of what could have been classed as incredulous stupidity, he took his meagre force of men to Oxford Street and confronted the angry mob. As luck would have it, Inspector Cuthbert's action became not an act of stupidity but an achievement that showed the very essence of British bravado. Cuthbert and his men, against overwhelming odds, baton charged the mob, and the rioters, seeing seventeen men armed with batons running towards them, ran and dispersed.

Two days after this incident, that became known as 'Black Monday', Scotland Yard heard a rumour that a mob was supposed to be gathering under cover of a dense fog, to continue the looting and destruction of property in the West End. They issued orders that all shops should be closed and barricaded against the coming onslaught. The mob turned out to be fictitious and this error by the police gave an even greater blow to the public's confidence in law and order.

An inquiry was set up following the fiasco of Black Monday and found that the police arrangements were entirely inadequate and at fault. Before learning of the committee's findings, however, Henderson resigned after seventeen years as commissioner. Sir Charles Warren took up the post and almost immediately his and the police's popularity took an even further decline. A riot broke out in Clerkenwell in late 1886, and Warren took the same attitude as Henderson by using heavy-handed police tactics to break it up.

In his report for 1886, published in early 1887, Warren stated: 'During the autumn attempts were made by unruly mobs to riot in the streets and Trafalgar Square, which proceedings were successfully coped with by the police.' This was in marked contrast to the Home Secretary's statement to parliament, when he said that the riots had 'exhausted the police and terrified the public'. However, the event that caused the most consternation and outcry against the police occurred in June 1887, and became known as the Cass case.

In today's courts, a lot would be made of an individual's civil liberties and a person's right to go where they wanted when they wanted without fear of arrest. In 1887, however, a young woman walking alone along the streets of London on her own after dark was more than likely a prostitute. Certainly Bowden Endacott believed the young woman he arrested on the night of 28 June was a lady of the night.

The woman in question was Elizabeth Cass and she was, in fact, a 23-year-old dressmaker. On the night she was arrested she had left work at about 8.30 pm and gone to Regent Street, supposedly to buy a pair of gloves and to see the illuminations celebrating Queen Victoria's Jubilee. While she was walking near Oxford Circus Bowden Endacott came up to her, took her arm.

'I want you,' he said.
'What?' she responded.
'I want you,' he repeated.

'What for?' she asked.
'I have been watching you for some time.'
'You have made a mistake.'
'No I have not. I have been watching you, and the other girl, and I wish I could have got hold of her.'
'But you have made a mistake,' she said. 'I was not with any girl.'
'Yes you were; she slipped behind. I wish I could have got my hand on her, she is worse than you are.'

Miss Cass asked where he was taking her and he replied to Tottenham Court Road Police Station. She again reiterated that he had made a mistake. Endacott said he had not and that he knew her well and had known her for some time. Miss Cass said that this was impossible as she had only been in London for three weeks. Endacott said that he had known her a lot longer than that. She asked him why he was arresting her and he said that it was for soliciting gentlemen. She asked if he would go with her to Mrs Bowman's in Southampton Row, with whom she lived, and who would tell him that he had made a mistake. Endacott replied that he could not go with her, as she would have to see the inspector first. Upon arriving at the police station, Elizabeth Cass was charged with being a common prostitute and put in a cell. Mrs Bowman arrived to bail her out and they both returned the next day to answer the charge before the magistrate.

The events that occurred during Miss Cass' arrest and charge, and the subsequent appearance before the magistrate caused huge controversy, with questions asked in parliament and a police inquiry. The outcome was a charge of perjury against Bowden Endacott that ruined his career in the Metropolitan Police and left him in debt.

On the day she was arrested Miss Cass had worked at Mrs Bowman's from 8.00 am until 8.30 pm. She said that she asked Mrs Bowman's permission to go out and left the house between 8.30 pm and 8.45 pm, without telling her mistress the reason for her departure. Elizabeth Cass said that she walked past the British Museum and into Tottenham Court Road, eventually finding herself at Oxford Circus. When she walked through a crowd at the corner of Oxford Circus and Regent Street, Bowden Endacott arrested her. He later stated that a gentleman had said to him, 'It is very hard that I should be stopped; it is the third time that I have been stopped in the street.' Cass, however, denied that anyone had spoken to the police officer. When they reached the police station in Tottenham Court Road, Sergeant Comber, the acting inspector, was fetched in and asked her name and whether she could read and write and she said yes. Then she was put in the cells until Mrs Bowman arrived at 11.00 pm to bail her out.

The next morning Elizabeth Cass and Mrs Bowman arrived back at the police station to appear before the sitting magistrate, Mr Newton. Endacott gave his evidence under oath and stated that he had seen Miss Cass on previous occasions, soliciting. His evidence was not corroborated by any other witnesses. Elizabeth Cass was called next and she vehemently denied that she had ever solicited or, indeed, had been in Regent Street when Endacott had said he had seen her on previous occasions. She stated that she had gone out to buy a pair of gloves on the night in question and to see the illuminations she thought were on to celebrate the Queen's Jubilee. Mr Newton then asked if she would like to call a witness on her behalf and she called Mrs Bowman, who was not sworn in. This was against the normal duty of a police court magistrate who was obliged to listen to evidence only under oath.

Mrs Bowman went on to say that Endacott had called at her house and said, 'I have come to see you about Miss Cass, your lodger.' Mrs Bowman told him that she did not keep lodgers and that Miss Cass worked for her and lived in. She said that she had been shocked when the officer had told her that Miss Cass had been arrested for soliciting and volunteered a statement to the effect that Miss Cass was her forewoman and had never left the house at night, until that evening, in the last three weeks. Mrs Bowman found Miss Cass to have an irreproachable character and to be a modest and proper young person, and she was certain she could not have done anything untoward. She went on to say that Endacott had been very rude in his attitude towards her.

Mr Newton, the magistrate, found the charges against Miss Cass were not supportable and dismissed them; but before this it was reported that when Mrs Bowman was giving her evidence Mr Newton said that she was out in Regent Street the previous night.

> Mrs Bowman: 'Yes, but for no bad purpose.'
> Newton: 'I say she was.'
> A shocked Mrs Bowman: 'I beg your pardon, Sir.'
> Newton: 'Don't beg my pardon; stand down.'
> Mrs Bowman, ignorant as to the language used in a courtroom: 'Stand where? What do you mean?'
> Newton to Miss Cass: 'If you are a respectable girl, as you say you are, do not walk Regent Street or stop gentlemen at ten o'clock at night. If you do, you will be fined or sent to prison. Go away and do not come here again.'

Newton clearly believed Endacott and thus branded Miss Cass a prostitute, even though the charges were not proven.

The next day Mrs Bowman sent the following letter to Sir Charles Warren:

> I beg to report a gross case of injustice to a young woman in my employ. On Tuesday night (28th), while passing down Regent-street, she was arrested by Police-constable Endacott, D R 42, and was charged at the police-station with accosting gentlemen. The police-constable said she was in company with a second female, and that they had accosted gentlemen. Both statements are false. Mr Newton thought it fit to 'caution' her when discharging her, and thus cast a lasting stigma and shame upon a poor, innocent girl.

The letter went on to say that the girl's mind had been 'quite unhinged' that she was injured by the charges and the reports of the case, and asked for an inquiry into the case. Mrs Bowman also sent a letter, dated 30 June, to the *Daily Telegraph*, addressed to the police authorities in reference to the arrest of Miss Cass and the attitudes of Constable Endacott and Mr Newton.

Her original letter to Sir Charles Warren arrived at the chief office in Scotland Yard on 2 July, and was acknowledged by a clerk. It was then sent to Mr Howard, the chief constable of the district, as was usual in cases of complaints against the police. Mr Howard did not see the letter until Monday 4 July. The following afternoon, 5 July, it was sent back to Chief Constable Howard, who immediately sent it to Sir Charles Warren. On Wednesday 6 July, Warren suspended Endacott from duty.

The day after, the circumstances of Miss Cass' arrest and details of the letter sent to Warren, reached the ears of the Member of Parliament for West Birmingham, Joseph Chamberlain, who asked the Home Secretary whether an inquiry would be held into the matter. The unpopular Henry Matthews, who was disliked by all parties, at first objected to an inquiry being held, as this newspaper report explains:

> It was beyond all question that this young woman had received a terrible and almost irremediable injury. But he could not help feeling that, placed as he was in a responsible position, he was not thus free, and he hardly thought the House of Commons, looking upon it as a corporate body, was free to pass any judgement upon the circumstances of the case, which were still in a broad sense *sub judice*. When he was first addressed about this case, and he took no blame to himself for it, he knew

> absolutely nothing beyond the report he received from the police magistrate consisting of his own statement and of the evidence in the case.... He was perfectly aware that it was in his power to direct the Commissioners of Police to inquire into the question whether or not the policeman had exceeded his duty. That, however, would be an inquiry of a most unsatisfactory kind, because it would be departmental and secret; in the second place, the evidence would be without the sanction of an oath; and in the third place it was an inquiry that could not exhaust the question whether or not the police constable had been guilty on a particular occasion of perjury.

Basically, he displayed a singular incapacity to grasp the true nature of the affair or to understand the indignation provoked in the public eye by the conduct of the police or the magistrate. He felt that his position made it impossible for him to inquire into the character of Miss Cass, nor the conduct of the police, and that it would have exceeded his function as Home Secretary if he inquired into the conduct of the magistrate. Matthews' continual do-nothing attitude lasted all the way through his career, as we have already seen in his later attitude towards Warren at the time of the Jack the Ripper murders.

During the ensuing debate in parliament, Joseph Chamberlain made an interesting observation by saying that the day after Miss Cass' arrest, in the same police court, another constable reported a similar case, in that he had heard a gentleman say it was very hard to be so accosted and was spoken to in Regent Street three times in that way in the course of half an hour. Chamberlain was of the opinion that it seemed to be some sort of police formula when arresting prostitutes to say that a gentleman had complained, and Endacott's statement to the effect ought to be viewed with some degree of suspicion.

The government eventually lost a vote upon a motion to adjourn the house by five votes, thus forcing Matthews to order that the commissioners of police hold an inquiry.

On Monday, 11 July 1887, the inquiry was opened at Scotland Yard, with Sir Charles Warren presiding and the Recorder of Lincoln, Horace Smith, acting as the assessor. Mr Grain and Mr F. M. Abrahams, instructed by Mr Bartrum, represented Miss Cass and Mrs Bowman and Mr St John Wontner represented Bowden Endacott. Mr Staples, the chief clerk of the commissioners, and Superintendent Cutbush of Scotland Yard were also present. Warren opened the proceedings by reading out the letter dated 7 July, from the Home Secretary, directing that an inquiry should be held into the circumstances of the arrest of Miss Cass. However,

Matthews had made a mistake in the letter; he stated that the arrest had taken place on 21 June instead of 28 June, thus giving us yet another indication of his sloppy attitude to this case and lack of attention to detail. Then, all of the relevant papers were introduced into the proceedings, including the charge sheet giving details that were taken when Elizabeth Cass was arrested:

> **Time.** 10.00 pm.
> **Age.** 23
> **Name and Address.** Elizabeth Cass, 11 Southampton-row, Bloomsbury, prostitute.
> **Charge.** Being a common prostitute, annoying male passengers for the purpose of prostitution at Regent-street.
> **Person Charging.** P.C. Endacott DR 42
> **Degree of Education.** Imp.

Warren asked whether the charge sheet was endorsed in any way after a case failed in the magistrate's court, and was told that it was not normal practice to do so. Therefore, the charge sheet remained as it was, classing Elizabeth Cass as a common prostitute. He was then reminded that he had written a letter to Sir James Ingham, (the chief metropolitan magistrate,) on the subject of the action of constables in the case of prostitutes, and this letter was read out in court:

> 4 Whitehall-place, SW., Oct. 23, 1886.
> Sir, — I shall be much obliged if you will bring the question as to evidence against prostitutes for soliciting before the quarterly meeting of the metropolitan magistrates on the 25th inst. On the 31st March 1883, you informed the Commissioners of Police that the magistrates were almost unanimous that the evidence of the constable alone would be sufficient when the person solicited showed by his conduct, in the presence of the constable, that he is annoyed by the solicitation. Since then there have been certain cases which lead me to suppose that there is no such unanimity among the magistrates at the present time, and it appears that some think that, according to 2 and 3 Vict., chap. 47, section 54, the annoyance should be proved by the person annoyed, the constables are quite uncertain how to act, and are placed in a most unfair and untenable position. While I am quite aware that persons will not as a general rule come forward to give evidence in such matters, and that if constables were to refrain from bringing cases forward on their own unsupported testimony great disorder would be likely to arise, especially in D Division, I still feel it is a question between the prospect of local disorders and the general efficiency of the police force.

> The present system and the uncertainties connected with it not only pave the way for the gravest charges being made against the police for blackmailing prostitutes, but also subject many most trustworthy constables to very great injustice, dishearten them for their work, and injure the efficiency of the police generally.
> I shall be glad if the magistrates can assist the Commissioners of Police by arranging for some common action on this matter in order to obviate present difficulties, and if in uncertain cases they will refrain from calling public attention to the police-constables, and if cases where they consider the constable has acted wrongly they will endorse the charge sheet, so that the Commissioners may know where the error lies.
> I remain you obedient servant,
> CHARLES WARREN.

Ingham's answer to Warren's letter was as follows:

> There can be no valid reason why more cogent evidence should be required against a prostitute that against a murderer or other criminal. The value of evidence must be tested by common sense and experience. No general rule applicable to all cases can be laid down. The magistrates suggest that the inspector who attends a court should make a report to the Commissioner upon cases touching the conduct of the police. Thereupon the Commissioner may, if he thinks the matter of sufficient importance, apply to the magistrate for permission to inspect the notes. If any serious mistake appears to be made; then application can be made through me for an explanation.

The circumstances Warren feared would happen were now occurring; a police constable was in danger of being charged with perjury on his evidence alone, as there had been no corroborative evidence brought forward during Elizabeth Cass' arrest. The inquiry had to decide whether Endacott had lied or not in his statement, on oath, that he had seen her on previous occasions.

Warren then asked the two sides on the case what action they proposed to take. Mr Grain, acting for Miss Cass and Mrs Bowman replied that they were there 'practically on an enquiry [sic] ordered by the government' and desired that 'the whole matter should be brought out to the best of [their] ability'. Thus, he added, 'We intend to tender the statements of Miss Cass and Madame Bowman, and then to call Endacott and other witnesses, in order that the court might put such questions as were thought fit, and that then I might be permitted to ask questions.' Warren jumped to Endacott's defence by saying that the inquiry was ordered by the

Home Secretary and Endacott would get no orders from him as his superior officer, and as far as he was concerned he was a free agent in the matter. In other words, if Endacott chose not to give evidence on his own behalf, that was okay.

Mr Wontner, on Endacott's behalf, said:

> Police constable Endacott has made a statement on oath, and for what he had said, if untrue, then he was criminally responsible. But I cannot see how we can mend matters by examining persons who were not under the obligation of oath and therefore I do not see what they were to do. If Constable Endacott was called upon to give evidence, I should have to exercise my discretion as to what advice I should give him; but as this inquiry is in the form of an investigation into the conduct of the constable by his superior officer, the responsibility should be upon the Commissioner rather than upon the constable.

The case continued with opening statements, and police officers giving their versions of events that happened when Elizabeth Cass appeared before the magistrate the following day, 12 July. She gave the following statement:

> I am twenty-four years of age, and was born in Grantham. I have been in several employments as a dressmaker, mostly near Stockton. I went into Madame Bowman's service on the 7th of June, as forewoman. In addition to my salary I had board and lodging. Madame Bowman has a niece, with whom I sleep. My duties end about eight o'clock as a rule, but often I am in the workroom afterwards. Before going to Madame Bowman I stayed with Mr and Mrs Tompkins, at 82, Durham Road, Manor Park, Forest Gate. I had been in Mrs Tompkins employ at Stockton. I know no one in London except Madame Bowman, Mr and Mrs Tompkins, and their families, and a person now at Shoolbred's. I have never lived in London before I came up to Manor Park, and was not in the least acquainted with the streets of London up till the 28th of June. I had never been out alone except on Saturday afternoons, when I went to Liverpool Street to take the train and go and visit Mr and Mrs Tompkins. Madame Bowman knew where I went. Before June 28 I had never been alone in Regent Street. I had never been there but once before, and that was one afternoon with Mrs Tompkins. Certainly I had never been anywhere near the streets at night. On Tuesday, the 28th June, Coronation Day, after working up till half past eight, I went out with the knowledge of Madame Bowman, who gave me leave. I wanted to go and purchase some gloves, but I was not going to any particular shop.

She then went on to describe the route she took towards Regent Street and the events surrounding her arrest, insisting that Endacott had been in error when he said he saw her with another woman and that he had seen her there before. Mr Wontner asked leave to reserve any questions he might have for Miss Cass so that 'he might institute inquiries, and prepare his questions which, put without inquiry might give pain.'

Mrs Bowman was then called and stated that Miss Cass had the highest references when she came into her employment. She went on to say that when Endacott had called on her to tell her of Miss Cass' arrest, he had been offensive in the way in which he had asserted that 'the girl had walked the streets night after night' and she described Mr Newton's conduct as, 'offensive, overbearing, and in every way insulting'. Further statements were taken from various police officers that were in the police station on the night of the arrest, and Mr Wontner then made an application that the case be adjourned in order for him to make enquiries respecting the persons involved in the case.

The inquiry continued on 21 and 22 July, with Mr Wontner complaining that although a great deal of correspondence had passed between himself and the Home Office since the adjournment nine days earlier, he had not had the means to make enquiries as to the character and antecedents of Miss Cass. This was because

> The pecuniary assistance Constable Endacott had applied for from Scotland Yard, had been refused, and therefore, under these circumstances, I am not in a position to carry into effect the views which I had before entertained of dealing with the case. I cannot, therefore, approach the inquiry into the matter in that full and complete manner in which I had desired to approach it.

Wontner went on to say that as Endacott had given his evidence under oath and the other witness had not, he would not put the constable forward to repeat the evidence he had already given. He then said that continuing the inquiry was simply continuing a farce.

Miss Cass' representative, Mr Grain, objected strongly to the inquiry being called a farce and Horace Smith, the assessor, added that if Wontner retired, the court would be able to hear witnesses whether they had given evidence on oath or not. Wontner reiterated by saying that Endacott had already given his evidence on oath, and that nothing had occurred that led him to alter his opinion of Miss Cass. He said, however, that he would ask some questions of Miss Cass and Madame Bowman and would call Constable Endacott.

Mr Grain said he proposed to recall Miss Cass and Madame Bowman, and ask a few questions of them which he had omitted to put on the last occasion. He went on to say the most searching enquiries had been made by Stockton police as to the antecedents of Miss Cass whilst resident in that town and they had revealed nothing but what redounded to her credit, and showed her to be a young woman of the highest respectability. Grain went on to say that he would call witnesses who would prove the respectability of Miss Cass.

At this stage Sir Charles Warren remarked that the enquiries at Stockton had not been instituted by the Scotland Yard authorities, as had been so stated in some newspapers. Mr Wontner told the court that assistance had been requested of Scotland Yard but it had been refused.

Miss Cass was then recalled to the witness box. It was noted that she was dressed all in black, just as she had been on the night she was arrested. Mr Grain asked questions of her and she said that before she came to London she was engaged to be married to Thomas William Langley, who was in the employ of a large firm of brass finishers at Burton, and that he was present and was ready to appear as a witness on her behalf.

Cross-examining her Mr Wontner asked her if she knew anyone who worked at Messrs Shoolbred's. Miss Cass replied that she did have a friend there, a gentleman named Suttle, but she was not going to see him on the night she was arrested. She had only gone out to buy a pair of gloves and thought she might also see some of the illuminations. Miss Cass said that she had walked down Oxford Street after leaving Mrs Bowman's and upon reaching Regent Circus (Street) had turned and walked down as far as Langham (Place), but, finding it dark, came back again. She said that she had been quite alone all evening. Mr Wontner asked her again about her friendship with the man named Suttle. Miss Cass said that he worked in the drapery department of Shoolbred's and that she had known him in the north of England before she came to London. When Wontner pressed her further about her relationship with Suttle, Miss Cass stated that there was not the slightest reason to suppose that anything wrong had taken place between them and that she believed he was a single man.

Other character witnesses were then called on her behalf, including Mr Tompkins who said that when he was a draper in Stockton Miss Cass worked for him as a draper and fitter and that he had excellent references from her first employer, Mr Carter.

He went on to say that from his own knowledge, Miss Cass was a highly respectable and modest young lady and that she was with him all the while he was in business at Stockton. When he left and came to London, she came to him at his house at Manor Park and stayed there for about six weeks, working with his wife, until she got a situation of her own. After she left to go to Madame Bowman's she came to stay at his house every Saturday to Monday.

Mr Wontner then said that PC Endacott was present, and could be called if necessary. Mr Grain replied that he would be glad if he was. Sir Charles Warren stood and said that the constable was not there by order of the chief commissioner, but entirely as a free agent.

Endacott, answering questions from Mr Grain, said that he was formerly in the Devon Constabulary, at Staverton. When Grain asked him why he had left the Devon police Endacott became vague. Eventually, after he was brought face to face with names, dates and faces he admitted that he was removed from the force on his own application as he had got a young woman into trouble at Staverton, although the case had not come to the attention of his superiors. The girl's name was Rogers, and she had lived with her brother, a miller, as housekeeper. He had been lodging there and had intercourse with the young woman, the result of which was a child. The matter had been settled by the payment of money before the child was born, and he had never seen the infant. It was then suggested that he had left the police force without giving notice, which Endacott strongly denied; he said he had given a month's notice after receiving the affiliation summons, which had been served upon him five or six months before the child was born. Another matter was then put to him regarding an incident involving a woman at Witheridge in Devon. As noted previously, Endacott lied and said that he had a cousin there, a policeman, of the same name as himself, and it was he who was involved with the woman. In reply to further questioning Endacott denied that he had had any trouble with women in London and said he was a married man with three children.

On the night he arrested Miss Cass, Endacott said that he saw another woman with her, soliciting gentlemen. There were other prostitutes about, but they all knew him and would not solicit in his presence, and he never arrested any of them anyway until they had solicited two or three times. The woman who was with Miss Cass was a trifle taller and fairer than her companion and when she saw him, she ran off. When Miss Cass had accosted three gentlemen, he arrested her.

In reply to further questions from Mr Grain, Endacott said that the first time he saw the two women they were going up Oxford

Street. As they walked along, leisurely, he did not take much notice of them until he saw them both take hold of a gentleman at the corner of Castle Street. His orders were to take them into custody.

Warren stood again and said that a constable had no orders: he acted upon his own discretion under an Act of Parliament.

Endacott continued, saying he had seen Miss Cass there two or three times before he arrested her, but could not state the exact times. His first impression of her was that she was a prostitute because of the manner in which she acted that night. He then said that it was a lie to say that when she was arrested Miss Cass said it was 'all a mistake'. He claimed she had asked him to not shew (show) her up in public, as she was not like a 'regular' girl. Endacott said he had been told that the other girl who had been with Miss Cass was a married woman. He went on to say that witnesses had come forward and they all confirmed they had seen Miss Cass walking the streets with another woman and that a man in a jeweller's shop in Great Portland Street had told him he believed Miss Cass to be 'a wrong 'un'.

Mrs Bowman was then recalled and said that it was the first time that Miss Cass had been out, and she believed that she had gone to Shoolbred's to meet a young man.

Miss Jane Scott (Mrs Bowman's niece) and Mrs Banks (Mrs Bowman's married daughter) then gave evidence, both of them agreeing that Miss Cass never went out at night, and that her behaviour was most exemplary.

Superintendent Draper, the chief of Endacott's division, was called and said that some time prior to the question being asked in the House of Commons, he had asked Endacott if he had any proof of his statements regarding Miss Cass. Endacott had told him that he knew a man named Wheatley, a joiner, who worked in the Euston Road and had witnessed the arrest. Wheatley had come to the station and made a statement on 4 July.

Wheatley was called and said that his name was James Wheatley, a carpenter and joiner of 4 William Street, Manchester Square. He said that he knew Constable Endacott by sight but did not know his name until this case occurred. Examined by Mr Wontner he said that on 28 June he was standing on the corner of Margaret Street (a turning out of Regent Street between Oxford Circus and Langham Place), at about 9.30 pm or 10.00 pm, when he saw the girl arrested. He had a closer look at her as he believed she was the same girl he had seen in the company of a fair woman whom he had seen before in Regent Street, talking to men. It was his belief that the fair woman was married as he had seen her in the Edgware Road with a basket and in the company of an elderly man, whom he believed was her husband. Since he had seen her with this older man, he had made it his business to look for her, as he knew that although she was married, she was a prostitute. Wheatley went on to say that at the time he made his statement to the police he was sure that the girl he had seen with the fair woman was Miss Cass, but he had a doubt now whether he was correct. He had seen Miss Cass arrested and he did say that from her general attitude and the way she walked with the policeman, there was nothing to indicate that she was of *that* class. He knew for certain that the fair woman was.

Mr Grain showed Wheatley a business card and asked him if he knew anything about it. Wheatley said it was the card he had given to the policeman, but then said that it was a copy of the card he had given to the constable. He went on to say that he had not called upon Mrs Bowman and left the card with her, nor did he know who had done so. Wheatley then said that he told Constable Endacott that a Frenchwoman (whom we shall meet shortly) was watching him. When asked if he knew Endacott socially, he said that he used the Cock Public House in Great Portland Street, (the present-day Cock Tavern at 27 Great Portland Street) and that he knew Endacott frequented this place, but he had not been there with him, or any prostitutes. He also vehemently denied that he had told someone that Endacott received money at night from prostitutes, in the form of a bribe, so he would not take them into custody.

The inquiry continued with the statement of a Mr Reeves, the manager of a jewellery establishment in Great Portland Street. Reeves stated that he knew Miss Cass to be what she was accused of, as he knew the fair woman she was seen with. This woman was named Mrs Frampton and she had told him that 'her friend Eliza' had been locked up, and he knew 'her friend Eliza' was Elizabeth Cass. Reeves then went on to say that Mrs Frampton lived in Carlisle Street; he knew this because he had been there with her. He had gone with a police officer to try and see if he could remember exactly where the house was but was unable to. Carlisle Street did not receive a good character at the hands of the police. He also said that Elizabeth Cass had accosted him on several occasions as she knew he was a friend of Mrs Frampton's.

Mrs Bowman was then recalled and was handed a card – a duplicate of that which Wheatley had given to the police as his place of business – 153 Euston Road. That card, she said, had been brought by a gentleman who represented the firm and he had come to warn her that a carpenter was concocting a story with the police to say that Miss Cass was known to them.

The assessor refused to allow this evidence, as uncorroborated third-person statements were not permitted. He said that many anonymous statements had been made to the inquiry; but these were also not allowed.

The inquiry then entered into an extraordinary phase. A Frenchwoman aged about 40 was introduced. Her name was given as Madame Fernande Pietra, or Pietri, for after she had given her full name she asked that neither her name nor her employment should be mentioned as it would injure her business, the inference being that she was the head of an establishment. A long discussion arose between the assessor, Warren and the prosecution and defence lawyers. Warren told Madame Pietra that she need not answer any question she chose not to, and that she was free to go anyway. Messers Wontner and Grain would not allow any statement to be made by her unless they were given the power to test it. Madame Pietra vehemently declared, with many protestations, that it would be on her conscience if she did not make a statement, and then said she would give the name of Botellier. She was employed at a dressmaker's, she said, in Regent Street, and lived in Titchfield Street; but was going home on 28 of June up Regent Street, 'on the side of the Langham' (the opposite side to the one on which the arrest took place), when she saw Miss Cass with a fair girl. They were close together, and they took hold of a gentleman's arm. She said Endacott pushed Miss Cass and then he took her. The other girl ran away. Madame Pietra went on to say that one of the girls was dark, and the other fair; the dark one having her hair cut almost 'like a boy'. (It had been remarked on in the press that Miss Cass had her hair cut thus.) She said that during the last two months she had often seen Miss Cass in the area, usually with another woman.

Mrs Bowman, Miss Cass, Mrs Tompkins and two other ladies were brought into court and Madame Pietra pointed out Miss Cass as the 'dark girl' she had seen.

Madame Pietra was about to speak of her impressions of work girl's habits when they were not at work when the assessor stopped her. She was told only to tell of what she knew of events that happened on 28 July, and, in reply to Mr Grain, she said that the gentleman whose arm Miss Cass held was an American who frequently walked up that way and went with bad women, but on this occasion he wanted to shake the girls off. She described him as about forty years of age and said that the fast women about there had a nickname for him (which was not given in court). She was asked when she had first heard about the matter and replied that her employees had been reading about the commotion in a weekly newspaper the following Monday, and were sympathetically inclined towards the girl. She went on to say that the girls she worked with did what they liked outside of work, although they were respectable. It seemed to her that the girl went to the station like a regular prostitute – quiet as a lamb, not, as an innocent woman would have done, by making a commotion.

Mr Grain then said: 'You seem to be well acquainted with the lives and habits of this class, madam?'

Madame Pietra replied laughing: 'I have been twenty years in England. It is quite a common thing to see these arrests in Regent Street at night.' When asked what she had been doing there at that time at night she replied that she was waiting for a dressmaker friend but declined to give her name.

The following day's newspapers picked up on the point in Wheatley's evidence when he had denied that he told someone that Endacott had been blackmailing prostitutes in order not to take them into custody. This was not the first time corruption of this sort had been spoken of in public. Warren had already taken the step of issuing the following police order on 19 July.

> PROSTITUTES: – In the absence of any legal opinion or decision on the subject, the Commissioner does not think that the police are justified in calling any woman a common prostitute unless she so describes herself, or has been convicted as such, and inasmuch as persons charged with offences frequently state their occupation incorrectly, and also do not necessarily again transgress the law after conviction; the Commissioner thinks it advisable that a Police Constable, while admitting that the Metropolitan Police District contains common prostitutes, should not assume that any particular woman is a common prostitute, although he may be perfectly convinced in his own mind that she is such. At the same time the Commissioner points out that, the Constable must be governed by the Act of Parliament, and if he at his own discretion chooses to call a woman a common prostitute, his justification will lie in the finding of the Magistrate.
>
> The offence of solicitation ... cannot occur without the presence of the inhabitant or passenger annoyed, who is capable of proving the annoyance, and, therefore, the Commissioner considers it desirable that a Constable should not, himself, charge any woman for solicitation, but should only arrest when she is formally charged by the person annoyed or solicited, or by some inhabitant or passenger who can prove the annoyance.
>
> If this course is pursued it will effectually dispose of the possibility of any person being able hereafter to charge the

Police with blackmailing prostitutes, as such a system cannot possibly exist when the Constable does not arrest on his own uncorroborated evidence. The Commissioner desires to say on the subject that he will institute the fullest enquiry into the allegations made by the public on the subject of blackmailing, and is quite aware that the Police Force court the most open and complete investigation. He has to observe, that as yet no evidence has been brought before him regarding this grave charge, and he remarks that the accusations have been hitherto made under assumed names, or by persons speaking from such positions that they cannot readily be required to show whether they have any foundation for their allegations, and the Commissioner thinks it desirable to assure the Police Force that during the time he has been in office no statement that any such system is in existence has been made to him. He is, of course, aware that isolated cases may exist just as the Police are aware that offences against the law are committed by persons in every grade of society, and in every body or community.

This order became the subject of considerable contention during the next twenty months. The Home Office pointed out that it had been issued in the absence of any legal opinion or decision and asked the commissioner to consult his legal advisers on the matter. Eventually the commissioner, James Monro, asked Wontner whether, under the Metropolitan Police Act, it was lawful for police to refuse to arrest unless annoyance to any particular inhabitant or ratepayer is proved or alleged, or unless the prostitute is formally charged by the person aggrieved.

Wontner's opinion was in direct conflict with the order, for he thought that it was obligatory for the constable to take action if he observed a breach of the law as a number of minor nuisances would occur unchecked unless the police took action.

This order possibly condemned many of Jack the Ripper's victims to death. At the height of the murders, the police were unable to arrest any prostitutes whom they felt might have been in danger, and keep them safe in custody for the night.

It was not until March 1889 that any change was made, after Monro addressed the Home Office and pointed out the difficult position in which the police were placed due to the divided state of public opinion on the matter of prostitutes. Monro thought the police order was ill-advised but that it would be better to let it become gradually obsolete than to attempt to define police action as a matter that should be left to the discretion of the constable.

The Home Office agreed and forwarded their papers bearing the following observations:

> The cases in which police ought to interfere are: – cases where a woman behaves riotously and assaults passengers, cases where a passenger complains of annoyance to a P.C., even though he declines to make a charge, cases in which women obstruct the footway and stop men whom they solicit. Arrests should be reserved for extreme cases where a woman will not move on.

The Home Office agreed that to issue new police orders would be inexpedient and that a gradual change would be better.

This was for the future though, and because Endacott followed the letter of the law at that time in arresting Miss Cass, he was fighting for his career and possible freedom.

In *The Times* on Thursday 28 July, the following brief report appeared:

> THE CASS INQUIRY –
> It is understood that the report of the Commissioner in the Cass inquiry was yesterday morning sent to the Home Secretary.

Bowden Endacott was to be prosecuted.

CHAPTER 3

Back in the Dock

The committal proceedings against Endacott began at Bow Street Police Court on Monday 9 August, before Mr Vaughan. An application was made by Mr J. P. Grain, with Mr F. Abrahams, instructed by Mr J. A. Bartrum, for a summons against PC Endacott for perjury alleged to have been committed in evidence given in connection with a charge preferred against Miss Cass.

Mr Grain opened by saying that the matter had created a great sensation and that although the perjury had occurred at Marlborough Street Police Station it was thought more becoming to apply at this court.

Grain said that the idea had occurred to him but that there were matters that did not come out at the inquiry and which would necessitate the attendance of officials at the court. He thought that it would, therefore, be advantageous for the case to be heard there. Vaughan granted the summons and fixed it for the following week.

Bowden Endacott appeared before Mr Vaughan at Bow Street Police Court on Tuesday 17 August, and pleaded 'Not Guilty' to a charge of wilful and corrupt perjury. Wontner appeared for his defence and Grain and Abraham for the prosecution.

Mr Grain opened by saying that he thought it right to put the magistrate in possession of the facts relating to the position in which he stood in conducting the prosecution, and he produced the following letter he had received on 10 August:

> Treasury, Whitehall, S.W., August 10, 1887.
> Reg., on the prosecution of Miss Cass, v Endacott, P.C.
> Sir – I am directed by the Secretary of State for the Home Department to communicate with you as the solicitor for Miss Cass, and on behalf of the Secretary of State to propose to you either – (1) that the Director of Public Prosecutions should take up the prosecution against Endacott already instituted by you, or (2) that the prosecution should be left in your hands, in which case the Government would undertake to pay Miss Cass such expenses as might be properly incurred by her, and the Secretary of State would recall the instructions already

given to me as the Director of Public Prosecutions. I shall be obliged if you will favour me with your decision at your very earliest convenience, in order that I may communicate it to the Secretary of State, that the proceedings commenced by you on behalf of Miss Cass at Bow Street may be carried on as speedily as possible.

I am, Sir, your obedient servant,

A. K. Stephenson, Director of Public Prosecutions.

Miss Cass, who had decided that she would prefer the case to be directed by her own solicitor, was called and gave a detailed account of her life. However, she omitted some very important details. Here is an extract from this account that can be compared with what was said later.

On the Sunday night before the jubilee she went out with Jane Scott and Mrs Bowman's sister to see the illuminations, and slept in the house as usual that night. On one occasion, about three or four o'clock in the afternoon, she was in Regent Street with Mrs Tompkins, but with that exception, prior to June 28, she had never been in Regent Street. It was not true that prior to June 28 she had been three times within six weeks in Regent Street. She had never been in Regent Street prior to the date mentioned with any woman except Mrs Tompkins on the occasion she had referred to. On June 28 she left off work at about half past eight, and spoke to Mrs Bowman, and received leave to go out. She left the house between half past eight and a quarter to nine. She did not tell Mrs Bowman her object in going out. Until she came to Mrs Tompkins she had never been in London and knew nothing of the streets.

Mr Vaughan asked why she had gone out that night, and she replied to buy some gloves. She repeated her claims that she had arrived at Oxford Circus and the exchange she had with Endacott when he accused her of being with another woman and that he knew her very well, and he took her to Tottenham Court Road Police Station. She said that she asked if they could stop by her mistress Mrs Bowman but was refused. Mr Vaughan asked her if she had spoken to any gentlemen in Regent Street. Miss Cass answered no, and also denied the allegation that she and another woman were taking hold of a gentleman's arm.

When she was cross-examined by Mr Wontner, Miss Cass said that she did not buy any gloves and that was not the only reason she went out that night, she also thought that there might be some illuminations. She was also quite sure that Endacott arrested her in Oxford Street and not Regent Street.

Mrs Bowman was called and confirmed everything that Miss Cass had said and added that when Endacott had told her of Miss Cass' arrest he had been extremely rude to her.

Other witnesses were called on Miss Cass' behalf and the case was adjourned.

The case continued on Friday 19 August, with other witnesses called who gave evidence. Wontner said that he wished to put one particular question to Miss Cass regarding an answer she gave to a certain question at the original inquiry. This was refused by the magistrate Mr Vaughan who told Wontner, 'You can put the question elsewhere. At present I decline to admit any question on evidence which has not been given on oath.'

Mr Grain said that that was the case on behalf of the prosecution and Mr Vaughan told Endacott that he was charged with perjury committed in his evidence given at Marlborough Street Police Court against Miss Cass, and administered the usual caution. He then told Endacott that he was committed to take his trial at the next sessions of the Central Criminal Court. Endacott's bail was set at two sureties in the sum of £20 each, a very large sum of money at the time.

On Tuesday, September 13 1887, the grand jury returned a true appeal against PC Endacott. In the afternoon Mr Besley, who with Mr C. F. Gill appeared for the defence, applied for a postponement of the case until the next sessions. In support of the application, Mr Besley read an affidavit signed by Wontner, the solicitor for the defence. It stated that in consequence of the action of the authorities in refusing to provide funds for the defence the defendant had been left to his own resources. Enquiries had recently been made on the part of the defence, and certain materials had been collected. Mr Besley said that it was essential that these materials should be sifted and determined into. There was no reason, he urged, that the case should be hurried on, as the defence declined to allow the prosecution to see the materials which had been collected.

Mr Grain said the Solicitor General had delegated him to conduct the prosecution and he opposed the application for postponement. The inquiry was one of a painful character to both parties – Miss Cass, who was now married, and Endacott. Grain continued by saying that the facts were now a matter of public record. However, counsel thought it right that every latitude should be given to Endacott's solicitor, Mr Wontner, and an adjournment of ten days was granted in order that Mr Wontner could make enquiries.

Mr Besley handed the notes of the materials referred to on the part of the defence to the learned judge. Mr Justice Grantham said he would read the notes and would give his decision on the application tomorrow morning.

The next day Mr Justice Grantham agreed to a postponement until the next sessions.

On 31 October the trial reached its final stage with the Solicitor General putting the case for the prosecution. He began by outlining the facts of the case to the jury, and in conclusion he pointed out that the question for the jury would be whether or not Endacott committed wilful and corrupt perjury in the evidence given by him at Marlborough Street Police Court on the hearing of the charge brought by him against Miss Cass.

Mr Crowe, the second clerk at Marlborough Street Police Court, was called as a witness and asked whether Endacott had been placed on special patrol duty. Crowe assumed that he had as Endacott had given evidence at the court on a large number of cases against prostitutes he had arrested.

It should be pointed out here that Endacott was in a very specialised job within the Metropolitan Police. Although he was a constable, he wasn't just an ordinary police officer; he was a member of what some would call the elite officers of the time, a reserve officer. In those days a reserve officer was always called out to perform duties on ceremonial occasions involving the Queen. A reserve officer was always on first call in any emergency and wore civilian clothing, not a uniform. Endacott would have been one of the first officers called to the scene to help out in patrolling the streets of Whitechapel as the murders progressed.

Miss Cass was then called to give evidence. I have reproduced a great deal of her testimony, albeit without the questions that were asked of her, as I believe that this proves that Endacott was correct in his assumption that she more than likely was prostituting herself when she was arrested. The police had decided to enquire whether Miss Cass could be examined by a doctor to ascertain whether she was as maidenly as she purported to be.

Her opening words completely changed the situation though.

When she came to the witness box, the Solicitor General began by asking her name:

> My maiden name was Cass. I have been married since the commencement of these proceedings. I am twenty-four years of age. Until the 27th April last I had spent my life mostly at Stockton ... I had never been to London. On that day I came

to London, and went to stay with Mrs Tompkins, at Manor Park, Forest Gate ... . While I was staying with Mrs Tompkins I came to town with her on two occasions to look for a situation. On one occasion I went to the city with her to the wholesale houses, and on one occasion to the West End, and we were in Regent Street at three o'clock in the afternoon. I had never been in Regent Street before the 28th June, except on that occasion. At the end of May I saw an advertisement of Madame Bowman's; it was on Whit Tuesday, May 31st... . On June 7 I went to Madame Bowman's and commenced my duties as forewoman... . On two occasions between the 7th and 28th of June I spent from Saturday till Monday with Mrs Tompkins at Forest Gate, leaving at four on the Saturday afternoon and returning at nine on the Monday morning. Once or twice I went to the post, which is at the bottom of the street, but came back immediately. On one Sunday I went to the city with Jane Scott after church in the evening. We came back to supper. With these exceptions I had not been out at all during the time I was with Madame Bowman. On the evening of June 28 ... I asked Madame Bowman's leave to go out, and, getting it, I went out between eight thirty and a quarter to nine. I was dressed as I am now, and I was alone. I went through Bloomsbury Square, passed the British Museum and into Tottenham Court Road, turning to the right, and then returning down Tottenham Court Road. When I got to the bottom of Tottenham Court Road, I noticed a jewellers shop there. I turned to the right and knew I was in Oxford Street. I went along as far as Peter Robinson's, keeping the same side. At Regent Circus I turned to the right and went as far as the church (All Souls, Langham Place.) I turned and came back to Regent Circus. I then turned to the left along the same side of Oxford Street. During all that time I had been alone. I had spoken to no one and no one had spoken to me. After I turned to the left in Oxford Street there was a little crowd at the corner, and when I had passed it Endacott came up, took hold of my arm. [She then reiterated the conversation she had with Endacott although added that when she said she had not been with another woman, he said 'Don't tell lies'.] I asked where he was taking me to. He said to Tottenham Court Road Police Station. I asked him to go to Madame Bowman's with me. By that time we had got out of Oxford Street and turned into great Portland Street. He said, 'I have known you some time.' I replied, 'You could not have done. I have only been in London six weeks.' He said he would not go to Madame Bowman's. I asked him not to take hold of my arm. He replied that he must or else I should tell them at the police station that he let me walk quietly. He asked whether Madame Bowman would bail me out. I said, 'Bail me out?' I know what bail meant, but that did not know that I should need it. No gentleman ever said in my hearing if that he had been stopped several times. At no time during that evening had I accosted or spoken to anyone. When I arrived at the police station Endacott spoke to another policeman, but I did not hear what he said. Endacott said to me, 'You don't know me, do you?' I said, 'No.' He said, 'I have known you some time.' At that time he was near me and looking at me. Endacott said he had known me for some time, about six weeks. I said he could not have done, as I had only lived in London three weeks. He said, 'You said six weeks just now.' I replied, 'I have been in London three weeks, but have been staying at Manor Park.' I next remember feeling giddy and I fell, and someone brought me some water, a chair also being brought for me. Another policeman said to me, 'Don't put yourself about, it will be all right.' When Sergeant Coomber came in Endacott spoke to him, and Sergeant Coomber took down what he said. Sergeant Coomber asked me my name and I said, 'Elizabeth Cass'. He asked whether I could read and write, and I said I could. A policeman standing by led me into a cell and Sergeant Coomber followed. I asked Sergeant Coomber if he would send for Madame Bowman, and he said he would. I was locked in the cell and remained there for about an hour. Madame Bowman then came. I did not see Endacott when I came out of the cell. Madame Bowman bailed me out. Next morning I went with Madame Bowman to the police court. Endacott was called as a witness against me and was sworn. Madame Bowman made a statement and I was allowed to go.

Cross-examined by Mr Besley, she defended her character against some rather damaging accusations:

I went to see Mrs Robertson at Trinity Square twice in May, the first time staying three days and the second a week. On the first visit I did not go out at all; and on the second visit I went out on Whit Tuesday in the afternoon. I took an omnibus bus to the Bank and walked to Madame Bowman's, Southampton Row, arriving there between four and five o'clock. I went direct. I remained at Southampton Row half an hour and returned to Trinity Square going over Westminster Bridge, arriving home at eight. I walked home. I went into a shop to buy some riband. That was the only time I went out while staying with Mrs Robertson. I was out one evening for ten minutes, and these are the only times I have been out in London by myself. I knew a young man named Arthur Settle at Shoolbred's, and I went there to buy the riband. This was after five in the afternoon – it was not so early as four. I went to Southampton Row first. I told Settle that I was staying at Trinity Square, and was going to see about getting a situation. He told me he could not leave business till seven thirty. I said I would come back. There was no one near enough to hear what was said. Settle was going to walk with me to Trinity Square. I returned at seven thirty, but had to wait till nearly eight for Settle. Between five and seven thirty, I was looking at the shops, and stayed in Tottenham Court Road the whole time. I did not go to Oxford Street. I did not go out of Tottenham Court Road. The visit with Mrs Tompkins to Regent Street was before then. I walked with Mr Settle to Trinity Square, arriving at about nine o'clock. I do not know what streets we went through from Tottenham Court Road to Westminster Bridge. I slept at Mrs Tompkins seniors, at Romford, about seven nights... . On the Jubilee night I went with Madame Bowman, her sister, and Miss Scott to see the illuminations. I heard there were to be illuminations on the night of June 28. On that night I did not tell Madame Bowman that I was going out to meet the young man at Shoolbred's. I did not tell her why I was going out. I went out to buy a pair of gloves and to see the illuminations. I did not make any enquires at Shoolbred's for Mr Settle. Most of the shops were closed, and I did not see any glover's shops. I went up Oxford Street to see the illuminations. I did not notice that the omnibuses and foot passengers were all going towards the city. The pavements were not very crowded. There was a small crowd at the corner of Regent Street, and I had just passed it when Endacott took me into custody. At the police station some water was brought me, but did not refuse to take it, nor did I say, 'If I want water I can ask for it.' Sergeant Coomber did not ask my occupation. I did not say to any constable, 'That man, [Endacott] has made a mistake. I have only been up that way twice.' As I was being put in the cell I asked them not to put me there. I did not say anything about bail. I told the policeman where I lived. I have never before made any statement in public about walking with Settle to Trinity Square. I know Jane Elizabeth Whitehead at Stockton. She was in the same situation as myself. I was on good terms with her up to my leaving Stockton. She did not say she would see me off by train, and I did not tell her that 'Bryan' was going to do so. I knew Bridget Costelloe, a barmaid at Stockton. I saw her on the Wednesday morning when I left Stockton. A friend of mine – Mr Bryan – was with me. He met me at Eaglescliff Junction. He joined the train at Eaglescliff to go to York. We arrived at York at one o'clock and we had luncheon. He had not a portmanteau. I left him at York and came on to London the same day. I knew he was married. I had known him for about a year. It was not an accidental meeting, but by a verbal appointment made on the Monday before. My father and brother saw me take my ticket and saw me off at North Stockton Station. This was the same day that I went to London.

I did not tell Whitehead that Bryan had bought me a satchel and gloves and was going to see me off. I had seen Bryan about twice a week for some time. Bryan did not give me a satchel, but he gave me a pair of gloves, a glove box, and a diamond ring. He gave me the ring just before I came away. My husband has it now. I never visited Mr Bryan's wife. Bryan never told me that he had been forbidden his wife's brother's house because of his acquaintance with me. Mrs Bryan came to town at Christmas. Mr Bryan did not ask me to cook a goose that he had won at a raffle on Christmas Day. I did not see him on Christmas Day. I met him on the Sunday after Christmas on the ice at Norton. I was not with him in any house. On Good Friday I went out for a drive in a dogcart to Castle Eden. I joined the dogcart at Norton. Bryan took me for the drive. No one else was in the dogcart. We met people who knew Mr Bryan. At Castle Eden we went to a hotel as the horse required rest, and Mr Bryan and I went into a private room. We had tea, and remained at Castle Eden an hour. We got back to Stockton at nine thirty. I met him on Easter Monday in consequence of a verbal appointment made on the Friday.

He got a trap, and we drove to Castle Eden. I drove all the way there, but not back. We went by the same road. I have driven with Mr Bryan to Seaton Carew. This was before going to Castle Eden. I have been twice to Seaton Carew. No one was with us. I was with him about an hour and a half. I once went by train to Seaton Carew. I did not know that his wife and family were in Redcar. I have never been to his house while his wife was away. I have often walked with him in the lanes near Stockton between eight and nine o'clock in the winter months when it was dark. A Mr Bevan did see me at eleven o'clock on night at Darlington Railway Station. A friend, Mr Turner, was with me. He was not kissing me. I had been to Darlington to do some work for Mary Costelloe. On passing a hotel I did not say, 'See how I will take him on.' I did not make any sign to anyone. I met a young man I knew in business named Turner, and went with him to the station. I had known Turner previously. I missed the train, but it was quite by accident. I went to my home in Stockton. Bryan sent me letters, but I do not know who brought them. I had known him for about a year. He is no relation. Miss Costelloe spoke to me about my acquaintance with Bryan. I did not tell her that I had broken it off with Langley, my husband, but it was not in answer to what Miss Costelloe said. I was married about August 17 last. We were married on Friday, [if she had been married on the Friday it must have been on 19 August] and my husband went to his work at Burton on the Sunday following. I have been living with my husband since Saturday last. I wrote to him.

I was born at Grantham. There was another family of the name of Cass at Stockton, but no relation of mine. I remember being introduced to Mr Simmons by Bridget Costelloe. I did not meet him afterwards, and I have never spoken to him since the introduction. It is not true that I made any appointment to go to his house on a Saturday afternoon. I have never been to his house. I have been working for Madame Bowman since my marriage. I renewed my engagement with Mr Langley after June 28.

Re-examined by the Solicitor General:

I have never walked nor been in any house with the man Simmons, except when Miss Costelloe introduced me to him in his shop. Turner was a commercial traveller. I had known him in business. I have never walked with him, except to the Darlington Station. No one spoke to me about it. I was introduced to Bryan by Bridget Costelloe. Miss Costelloe and I were walking down the High Street and she introduced me to him as a friend. She did not know his name. I did not know he was a married man till three months afterwards ... . I was never in a bedroom with Bryan at Castle Eden or anywhere else... . There was never any immoral relation between Bryan and myself. I have told my husband about the ring being given, and all these matters. Before June 28 my husband was in employment at Burton, and is still so. I remained in my situation at Madame Bowman's. I got to London the same day as I started from Stockton and I did not stay with anyone else. With the exception of the shop at York, where we went to get refreshments, I never went into any place with Bryan ... . I have known the young man Settle for five years. I knew him at Stockton. He is a Draper. While I was waiting for him, after I had been to Shoolbred's, I did not go out of Tottenham Court Road. I did not know the names of the streets in the neighbourhood. Settle walked with me to Mrs Robertson's in Trinity Square. At the police station I asked them to send for Madame Bowman, both before and after Sergeant Coomber came in.

Mrs Bowman was the next witness called, and gave evidence as to when Cass came into her employment and when they went out together. She was then asked about the type of establishment she ran, the inference being it was some sort of brothel. Madame Bowman indignantly and emphatically denied the suggestion, and Mr Justice Stephen observed that such questions ought not to have been put without good grounds.

Further witnesses were called to back up Elizabeth Cass' story of her time living in London, and the court then adjourned until the next day. Endacott was bailed on the same surety as before.

Elizabeth Cass' story gives us great insight into her character. She could have been telling the truth when she said that there was never any immoral relation between her and Bryan, although it does seem unlikely.

The final day of the trial was Tuesday, 1 November 1887. The first prosecution witness called was Elizabeth Ann Tompkins, who confirmed the evidence of Elizabeth Cass as to how long she had been in London and her whereabouts whilst there. However, when Mr Gill began to cross-examine her as to the evidence given by her at Scotland Yard, Mr Justice Stephen interrupted the proceedings by asking whether the inquiry was held under any authority. Mr Gill replied that it was held as a result of a letter written to the Home secretary by Madame Bowman. Mr Justice Stephen then asked what authority the Home Secretary had to order such an inquiry. Gill replied that he did not know. Mr Justice Stephen then made a statement that showed his attitude towards the case in general, and whilst his views and those he gave in his summing up were entirely within the framework of the law, it seems that because of the anti-police publicity the case had aroused he was perhaps trying to end it as expediently as possible. He said:

> Certainly he has no legal authority. The whole affair was a purely voluntary inquiry into what might turn into a criminal case at the insistence of a private person. That I must say is a very inconvenient way of administering justice. However, we have nothing to do with that. I can understand that if a police officer is said to have misconducted himself it may be proper for an inquiry to be held by his superior officers, but that would only be for purposes of police discipline, and might terminate in dismissal. But it is very inconvenient if there is to be a criminal inquiry afterwards that the preliminary investigation should be conducted otherwise than in the manner provided by law. You see this inquiry, which has taken place, is hard upon the person who is charged, and it places witnesses in a false position. This present witness was not on her oath, and she might naturally think she was justified in not bringing in the names of her friends. That prejudiced the case of the person to whom the inquiry related. However, as I have said, we have nothing whatever to do with that; we must take it as it comes.

Edward Walford, a draper's assistant, was the next witness called. He said that on the night of the arrest he had occasion to go to Davies Street, Berkeley Square, for a panel and returned by way of Oxford Street on the north side. He had noticed Miss Cass about twenty or thirty yards ahead of him when Endacott arrested her.

He said she did not speak to any gentleman and was not accompanied by any other girl. After the arrest he followed Endacott for some distance up Great Portland Street as he had not seen Miss Cass do anything wrong. No one had spoken to Endacott whilst he had been making the arrest, nor afterwards.

Officers that were on duty at Tottenham Court Road Police Station were called to give evidence into the events that occurred when Endacott and Cass arrived there. The Solicitor General then said that completed the evidence for the prosecution. Mr Besley said that he should only call character witnesses and Mr Justice Stephen asked the Solicitor General where was the corroboration which was necessary to support the assignment of perjury.

The Solicitor General contended that Walford's evidence corroborated the evidence of Miss Cass. He went on to say that one of the statements of Endacott on which perjury was assigned was that he saw Miss Cass catch hold of two gentlemen, one of whom said 'it is very hard that I should be stopped'.

A long discourse took place between Mr Justice Stephen and the Solicitor General as to what proof there was that Miss Cass had been in Regent Street on a number of occasions before the arrest. He pointed out that Endacott stated that he had seen her there three times before, and that was in the statement upon which perjury was alleged.

Mr Justice Stephen acceded that there may be some corroboration on that point, but that was for the jury to decide. He asserted that the only assignment of perjury that the jury could go into was whether Endacott committed perjury in saying that he had seen Miss Cass in Regent Street 'three times during the last six weeks'.

The Solicitor General asked whether his Lordship believed there was no corroboration as to the other parts of the case. Mr Justice Stephen said yes and added that the material part of the charge was that he saw her accosting men.

The Solicitor General consulted with the other members of the prosecution counsel and then said:

> I think, having regard to the intimation from your Lordship, that I will not address the jury upon the residue of the charge. Of course, if the whole case had been in your Lordship's judgement sufficiently supported to have gone before the jury, I should have gone to the jury upon it; but if it is to be limited under your Lordship's direction to the question whether Endacott did or did not see her three times in Regent Street, I do not think I can pursue the matter further. I quite feel the force of the observation that it may have been a matter of mistaken belief on

his part; and while I regret to some extent this course, I do not think it would be consistent, after your Lordship's observations, for me to ask for a verdict on the question left.

Mr Justice Stephen then made his final summing up for the jury in reply to the Solicitor General:

Nothing remains for me but to direct the jury that the man must be acquitted upon the whole charge. In doing so I must make some observations in explanation of the position in which we are placed ... .

In the case of perjury ... there is a rule, which ... may be briefly expressed in these words: – 'If, upon a trial for perjury, the only evidence against the defendant if the statement of one witness contradicting the oath on which the perjury is assigned, and if no circumstances are proved which corroborate such witness, the defendant is entitled to be acquitted.' That I believe to be the law of the land, and I may observe that that is stated less favourably to the prisoner than it usually is stated, because it is usually said that you cannot convict a man for perjury upon the evidence of less than two witnesses. There have been many cases in which a man has been convicted for perjury corroborated by circumstances not directly connected with it, but leading up to it. Suppose, for instance, it had been said that Endacott had admitted that he had told a lie that would do. Or, suppose you have proof that he had given evidence one way on one occasion and another way on another. But let us consider how the matter stands – and I wish to state this in order that my views as to this case, which has attracted considerable attention, may not be misunderstood. Substantially, what Endacott is charged with is that he, for some reason or another, arrested Elizabeth Cass in an arbitrary and tyrannical manner when she was doing no harm whatever. He says, in substance, on oath that he arrested her on account of what he saw, and that he did what he was justified in doing – not only justified, but what his duty as a police officer imperatively required that he should do. Now, what is the evidence that what he said it was not true? Simply the contradiction by the witness Cass. I will not say one word on the subject of that contradiction. I will merely say that in almost every case, which one has to try in a Court of Justice, whether civil or criminal, when any person's interests are strongly engaged, we almost always get contradictions. We have I cannot tell how many cases which are I have tried under what is called the Criminal Law Amendment Act in which the prisoner himself has been called as a witness, but he is never called unless he is prepared fully to contradict the charges made against him. In many cases that contradiction finds no weight at all in the eyes of the jury, although in some cases I have known men show their innocence by swearing to it under circumstances of a particular kind. But, on the other hand, I have known men convicted on the evidence of a single witness, when they swore positively that it was false. If you were to allow the oath of a person taken before a magistrate to convict of perjury, the effect would be that in a very little time you would have all the police in London committed for perjury. Nothing is more common than to hear a man, when asked whether he has not been previously convicted, answer, 'Yes; but I was quite innocent of the charge.' In this particular case it is not my duty to give any opinion; but I will just make one or two remarks in justice to the constable, which ought to be borne in mind. In the first place, there is considerable room for a mistake on the part of the constable; and what would have to be proved in order to convict of perjury is not merely the mistaken apprehension, but wilful perjury. It occurs to me as a possible thing that a man walking along the streets where there were many passengers might very well take the wrong woman, especially as she passed through a small crowd of people at the time. If there was a mistake of that kind, it would be a cruel injustice to convict a man of perjury. That would have been a subject to which I should have had carefully to direct your attention but for the course which the Solicitor General has taken, by which I am relieved of a necessity of saying anything about her being in Regent Street. But gentlemen just consider. Let us suppose that he had made a mistake about it. It must not be forgotten that his evidence was given in such a summary way and so shortly that he was not cross-examined. It was natural that the young women should not know anything about cross-examination. He had no opportunity of qualifying or setting himself right upon the statement with respect to which the perjury is assigned. If he had been cross-examined he might have had fair play. I do not say there has been any want of fair play in the conduct of the case, for it has been tried with perfect fairness. If Elizabeth Cass had been treated in this manner in consequence of the evidence she has given here, perjury might have been assigned against her, as she made one or two mistakes, but I am bound to say that she has given her evidence with extreme frankness and there was no perjury as far as I can see. That she still showed some want of candour in not admitting at once the receipt of the diamond ring from Bryan, but it would have been a cruel thing to snap a verdict of perjury against her in consequence, and it would be hard to convict this man because he said something which might have been a mistake. Your duty will be to acquit the prisoner.

With these words Mr Justice Stephen thus brought to an end one of the most controversial cases the country had known at the time.

After the case, Elizabeth and Thomas Langley moved to Burton upon Trent where they purchased a house with money obtained by Elizabeth who had sold her story to the press. They lived at 120 Shobnall Street in Burton for the rest of their lives and raised five children: Charles, Marjorie, Doris, Tom and Alfred. Thomas died in 1948, aged 90, and Elizabeth died in 1956 aged 93.

After the Cass case, Endacott's superiors in the Metropolitan Police decided that it would be better if he were taken off the streets and out of the public eye. He was assigned to permanent guard duty at the British Museum for the rest of his career. Some would say this was a cushy job, but Bowden was a police officer, a man of the streets, not a security guard. The trial had also left him seriously in debt. During June and July of 1888, he still owed his solicitors just over £250 in unpaid fees – a great deal of money in those days. Although a defence fund had been set up for him, not quite enough money was raised and, as we have already seen, his resentment against prostitutes must have been immense and there was one thing that gave him an advantage in his lust for revenge, he was still classed as a reserve officer and was called in to patrol the streets of Whitechapel during the murders. He had the motive and the opportunity to take his revenge on those who had ruined him – the prostitutes of London.

CHAPTER 4

Martha Tabram – Murdered 7 August 1888

The first murder I will examine is that of Martha Tabram. Although most researchers believe that she was not one of the Ripper's victims – and thus not one of the canonical five – as she was murdered before Mary Ann Nichols, in light of the later murders and the similarity of her injuries to these women, some police officers of the day believed that she was, in fact, the serial killer's first fatality.

Martha Tabram was a 39-year-old prostitute who lodged at 19 George Street, Spitalfields. She had been born Martha White on 10 May 1849 at Marshall Street, London Road, Southwark. At the time of her death, she was the estranged wife of Henry Samuel Tabram whom she had married on Christmas Day in 1869. Henry was a foreman furniture packer who lived in East Greenwich. He and Martha had separated in 1875 because of her drinking. At first, he paid her a 12/- (60p) weekly maintenance until he 'had found out how she was going on' – she had turned to prostitution – and he reduced the payments to 2/6d (12½p). In response, Martha took out a warrant against him and had him arrested. In 1879, however, Henry found out that she was living with a man named William Turner, and stopped paying altogether.

Martha and William lived together on and off for ten years. William, a carpenter by trade, was, at the time of Martha's death, making a living as a street hawker. He had left Martha from time to time, usually because of her drunkenness, saying at her inquest, 'If I gave her money, she generally spent it on drink. In fact, it was always drink. When she took to drink, however, I usually left her to her own resources, and I can't answer for her conduct then.'

The pair had been lodging with a Mary Bousefield, at 4 Star Street, until about three weeks before Martha's death. They left owing Mrs Bousefield two weeks' rent. Mrs Bousefield and her husband William, a woodcutter, later described Martha as a match seller.

Martha then went to live in lodgings in George Street, and William, who had tired of her drunkenness again, went to stay at the Victorian Working Men's Home in Commercial Street. On Saturday, 4 August 1888, William and Martha met in Leadenhall Street near Aldgate Pump. William gave Martha 1/6d (7½p). They separated, and William never saw Martha alive again.

Four to five months before her death, Martha had made friends with a woman named Mary Ann Connolly who was also known as 'Pearly Poll' or 'Polly'. An unmarried 50-year-old prostitute, she had been living at Crossinghams Lodging House – otherwise known as The Round House – which was situated at 35 Dorset Street. Crossinghams was a typical lodging house of its time where a bed sharing with someone else could be had for 4d a night and the whole bed could be rented for 8d. It was frequented by many of the characters associated with the Whitechapel murders.

On the evening of Bank Holiday Monday, 6 August 1888, Martha and Polly went out drinking and were seen from time to time in various public houses in the area until they arrived at the Two Brewers, which was situated until recently in Brick Lane. There they met two guardsmen, a corporal and a private. They drank with them in various other public houses, including the White Swan on Whitechapel High Street. Then, at about 11.45 pm, the party split up. Pearly Poll and the corporal went into Angel Alley, which is situated off Whitechapel High Street, for sexual intercourse leaning against a wall. Martha and the private went into George Yard (now Gunthorpe Street), which is a few yards away from Angel Alley. Polly left the corporal at the corner of George Yard at about 12.15 am on 7 August and went home. At about 2.00 am, 32-year-old PC Barrett of H Division, who had been in the Metropolitan Police service for five years, saw a young Grenadier Guardsman in Wentworth Street, which is situated at the north end of Gunthorpe Street. The guardsman told him he was waiting for a 'chum who had gone off with a girl'.

At 3.30 am, a man named Alfred Crow, a cab driver who lived in George Yard Buildings, a tenement block that had been converted from an old weaving factory, noticed what he believed was a tramp sleeping on the first-floor landing. John Saunders Reeves, a waterside labourer, left his residence, 37 George Yard Buildings, at 4.45 am. He came down the stairs and found the body of Martha on the landing. Immediately he went out to find a policeman and returned with PC Barrett. Another constable soon appeared on the scene, and he at once went to the surgery of Dr Timothy Robert Killeen at 68 Brick Lane. Dr Killeen, who arrived at the scene at about 5.30 am, estimated that Martha had died about two hours earlier. If we can assume that Alfred Crow was correct in his sighting of what he thought was a tramp asleep at 3.30 am then

Dr Killeen must have been slightly out in his estimation, or Martha had only just been murdered when Crow noticed the body.

Upon examining the body, Dr Killeen found thirty-nine stab wounds, including five in the left lung, two in the right, one in the heart, five in the liver, two in the spleen and six in the stomach. Her breast, stomach, and private parts seemed to have been the principal targets. He thought that a right-handed person had inflicted at least thirty-eight of the wounds. He stated that the heart was rather fatty and that the one stab wound there would have been sufficient to cause death. He thought that the wounds generally might have been inflicted with a knife, but such an instrument could not have inflicted the wound that penetrated the chest-bone. His opinion was that at least one of the wounds in the sternum had been caused by some kind of dagger.

Polly Nichols was questioned by the police, but then disappeared. Sergeant Eli Caunter, a 36-year-old police officer of eighteen years' service, eventually found her living with her cousin, a Mrs Shean, at 4 Fullers Court, Drury Lane. Polly was taken on an identity parade of Scots Guards at the Tower of London but did not identify the men she and Martha had been with. She then claimed that the men had white cap bands, which meant they were possibly members of the Coldstream Guards who were stationed at Wellington Barracks in Birdcage Walk. At a further identity parade, she picked out Guardsmen George and Skipper. Both of the soldiers were able to establish firm alibis, however, and the police decided that Pearly Poll was not willing, for reasons known only to herself, to give them any help in tracing the murderer.

The identity of the guardsman that PC Barrett spoke to at 2.00 am was never established and it is possible that his 'chum' was with a completely different prostitute, and not Martha Tabram. If they were the same two guardsmen that Polly and Martha had been drinking with, why were they there nearly two hours later? The mystery of exactly where Martha went and what she did between the time Pearly Poll left her and the time she was found murdered has never been solved.

Shortly after the crime, Polly and two other women, Elizabeth Allen and Eliza Cooper, who also lived at Crossinghams Lodging House, told the police about a certain man they suspected who lived not far from Buck's Row. The police enquiries proved fruitless.

CHAPTER 5

Mary Ann Nichols – Murdered 31 August 1888

The first of the five generally accepted Ripper victims was Martha Tabram's drinking friend and fellow prostitute, Mary Ann 'Polly' Nichols. She was the first victim to be deliberately mutilated.

A lot is known about Polly Nichols. She was born Mary Ann Walker on 26 August 1845, in Shoe Lane off Fleet Street. Her father, Edward Walker, was a locksmith who later became a blacksmith. Polly's mother's name was Caroline, but by the time of the young woman's murder, her father was living at 16 Maidswood Road, Camberwell on his own, so we must assume that he was a widower.

In 1864, Polly married William Nichols. The marriage took place on 16 January, at St Bride's Parish Church, Fleet Street. The service was conducted by Charles Marshall, the vicar, and was witnessed by Seth Havelly and Sarah Good. St Bride's was known as the printer's church, so William, being a printer, would have married there.

The couple lived in William's house in Bouverie Street briefly, before moving to 131 Trafalgar Street, Walworth, to live with Polly's father. They stayed here from 1865 until 1875. They then moved to 6D Peabody Buildings, Stamford Street, Blackfriars Road, Lambeth, where they lived until 1881, paying a rent of 5/6d (27½p) a week.

They had five children: Edward John, born 1866; Percy George, born 1868; Alice Esther, born 1870; Eliza Sarah, born 1877, and Alfred Henry, born 1879.

After Eliza was born in 1877, the marriage started to fall apart. This was due to a brief affair and elopement William had with the woman who had assisted Polly in her confinement with Eliza. Polly and William separated in 1880, with Polly's father spreading the story that it was because William had been having an affair. Polly left the matrimonial home and William, whilst not denying the allegation that he had been having an affair, stated that it was not the cause of her leaving, saying, 'the woman left me four or five times, if not six' and claimed his dalliance took place after she had left. It is obvious that there was disharmony within the household and the eldest son, Edward John, refused to live with his father and went to live with his grandfather, with William continuing to bring up the other children on his own. It is also believed that by 1877 Polly had started to drink heavily although William never used this as a reason against her.

Polly's movements after she and William separated are well documented. Between the marriage break-up in September 1880 and March 1883, Polly spent most of her time in the Lambeth Workhouse. In 1882 William, who had been paying Polly 5/- (25p) a week allowance, found out that she had been prostituting herself and refused to give her any more money. The parish authorities tried to collect the allowance on her behalf but he blocked this by saying she had deserted him, leaving him with the children. He won his case after establishing that she was now living as a common prostitute.

Polly continued to live in the workhouse until March 1883, when she moved in with her father at 16 Maidswood Road, Camberwell. At the later inquest into her death he testified that she was 'a dissolute character and drunkard whom he knew would come to a bad end'. He went on to say that whilst she was not a sober person, she was not in the habit of staying out late. Nevertheless, her drinking caused friction between them and in May 1883, they had a big row. Polly left the house the next morning and went back to the workhouse where she stayed for about a month.

Then Polly met and began cohabiting with a man named Thomas Stuart Drew, a blacksmith who had a shop in York Mews, 15 York Street Walworth. They stayed together for four years, until October 1887. During this time, in June 1886, Polly attended her brother's funeral. He had burned to death when a paraffin lamp exploded. At her inquest, Polly's family said that she was respectably dressed, so it is possible that she had given up prostitution whilst she was living with Thomas Drew. In October however, Polly and Thomas split up. It is not known exactly why, but we must assume it was because of her drinking. Polly moved back to the workhouse and stayed there until May 1888. It is during this time that she met Mary Ann Monk, who would eventually identify her body for the police. Monk is described as a young woman with a 'haughty air and flushed face'.

It was common practice at the time for workhouses to find domestic employment for their female inmates and Polly was no exception. On 12 May, Polly left the workhouse to begin work as a servant in the home of Samuel and Sarah Cowdrey.

Samuel Cowdrey was a 61-year-old clerk of works, working for the police department. His wife was a year younger. They were described as upright citizens, being very religious and teetotallers and they lived at 'Ingleside', Rose Hill Road, Wandsworth.

While she was working for the Cowdreys, Polly sent a letter to her father. It says a lot about the depravity she was used to and the situation she now found herself in:

> I just right [sic] to say you will be glad to know that I am settled in my new place, and going all right up to now. My people went out yesterday and have not returned, so I am left in charge. It is a grand place inside, with trees and gardens back and front. All has been newly done up. They are teetotallers and religious so I ought to get on. They are very nice people, and I have not too much to do. I hope you are all right and the boy has work. So goodbye for the present.
> From yours truly
> 'Polly'
> Answer soon please, and let me know how you are.

Perhaps Polly was trying to change when she talked about the Cowdreys being 'teetotallers' and religious and adding 'so I ought to get on'. We can only surmise that she felt bad about the arguments she had had with her father and was trying to make amends and begin a new life. She may of course just have been being sarcastic.

Her father Edward wrote a reply but never received one back. We can assume that by 12 July, Polly was tired of the life she was leading and left, or rather ran away from, the Cowdreys, stealing clothing from them at the same time. The clothing was worth £3.10s (£3.50).

Until 2 August, Polly once again lived in a workhouse, before moving into a common lodging house at 18 Thrawl Street, Spitalfields where, for the sum of 4d, she shared a room with four other women. The room was described as being surprisingly neat and tidy. One of the other women was called Emily (Nellie), or Ellen Holland. Nellie was 50 years old and by October 1888 she had two convictions for being drunk and disorderly. On 24 August, Polly moved to a lodging house known as the 'White House', situated at 56 Flower and Dean Street. In this doss house, men were allowed to share a bed with women.

At one time or another three of the Ripper's victims had lived in Flower and Dean Street. Most of the lodging houses in the area catered for prostitutes and in 1883 Flower and Dean Street was described as 'perhaps the foulest and most dangerous street in the whole metropolis'. The area encompassing Flower and Dean Street and Thrawl Street was known as the 'evil quarter mile'.

In 1889, Margaret Harkness, using the pseudonym John Law, wrote a book *In Darkest London,* which gave an accurate account of what life was like in Flower and Dean Street. The doss house she spoke of was a cover for a thieves' kitchen and Margaret Harkness conveys the details with obvious familiarity: 'They were a savage looking set of men. No policeman ever entered alone into their kitchen.'

Thursday, 30 August 1888, a downpour of heavy rain had ushered out one of the coldest and wettest summers on record. By the time night came, the rain was sharp and frequent and accompanied by peals of thunder and flashes of lightning. It was the perfect night for a Victorian melodrama acted out upon a stage, but no one could have envisaged the true horror of what was about to begin.

At about 11.30 pm, Polly Nichols was seen walking down Whitechapel Road, probably soliciting for trade. By 12.30 am, she was seen leaving the Frying Pan public house which stood on the corner of Brick Lane and Thrawl Street. She then went to the lodging house at 18 Thrawl Street, a bit worse for drink. At about 1.30 am the deputy of the lodging house told her to leave, as she did not have the 4d required for a bed for the night. On leaving, Polly told him to save a bed for her, saying, 'Never mind! I'll soon get my doss money. See what a jolly bonnet I've got now.' She pointed to a little black bonnet that no one had seen before, and staggered away laughing.

On the night these events took place two fires broke out in London Docks. Ellen Holland had gone down to the docks to watch the fires, which erupted in Messers Gibbs & Co., engineering works in Shadwell dry dock. The fires destroyed a sailing ship spar and rigging before igniting 800 tons of coal at Gowlands Coal Wharf, which burned until late in the morning.

Whilst Ellen was walking back from the docks, she bumped into Polly outside a grocer shop on the corner of Whitechapel Road and Osborn Street. Polly had just come down Osborn Street. Ellen said that the time was 2.30 am as she had heard the clock striking on the church tower. She noticed that Polly was very drunk and tried to persuade her to come back with her to the lodging house in Thrawl Street, but Polly refused, saying that she had earned her doss money three times over that day and had drunk it all away. She told Ellen that she would return there after one more attempt to find trade. The two women talked for seven to eight minutes, then Polly said, 'it won't be long before I'm back' and left, walking

Mary Ann Nichols – Murdered 31 August 1888

east down Whitechapel Road. Ellen was the last person, apart from the murderer, to see Polly alive.

At this time, the services of a destitute prostitute such as Polly could be had for 2d or 3d, or even a stale loaf of bread. The usual rate was 3d though, as this was the price of a large glass of gin.

Buck's Row is situated about ten minutes' walk from Osborn Street; its only illumination was from a single gas lamp placed at the far end. At 3.15 am PC John Thain, 96J, walked down the row as part of his normal beat and saw nothing unusual. At about the same time, Sergeant Kerby passed down the row and saw nothing. At approximately 3.45 am, Charles Cross, a carman who lived in Doveton Street, Cambridge Heath Road, Bethnal Green, was on his way to work at Pickfords in Broad Street. His route took him down Buck's Row, which at that time was a long straight cobbled street that ran parallel with Whitechapel Road. The row stretched from Brady Street to Baker's Row (today's Vallance Road).

Cross entered Buck's Row from Brady Street and as he passed Essex Wharf which was situated on the north side of the street until its demolishment in 1990, he noticed what he thought was a tarpaulin on the opposite side of the street. He went to examine it thinking it might have been worth salvaging and was shocked to find it was a woman with her skirt pulled up. Within a few moments another man entered the row from Brady Street. He was Robert Paul, a carter, who lived at 30 Foster Street, Whitechapel and who worked in Corbetts Court on the corner of Hanbury Street and Commercial Street.

Cross called him over to examine the woman, and Paul, feeling her hands and face said, 'I think she's breathing, but it's very little if she is.' Paul then decorously attempted to pull the woman's dress back down over her legs. It is noteworthy here that possibly Cross and Paul decided not to get involved because instead of going into Brady Street and looking for PC Thain, whom they must have known patrolled the area, they carried on their way to work. It wasn't until they had crossed Baker's Row and entered Hanbury Street that they come across PC Jonas Mizen, 55H, a 40-year-old officer with fifteen years' service on the force.

There are contradictory statements as to what exactly Cross is supposed to have said to Mizen when they met and I am led to wonder whether Cross and Paul told the exact truth about the events that happened in Buck's Row. Constable Mizen stated at the inquest that when Cross spoke to him, he said, 'You are wanted in Buck's Row, by a policeman, a body has been found'. Cross, on the other hand, vehemently denied that he had used the words 'by a policeman'. I cannot for one minute imagine that an officer with fifteen years' experience would mistake what he had been told, especially after finding out the severity of the crime. My views are that there was someone else in Buck's Row with Cross and Paul, and that person was Bowden Endacott. Although I will never be able to prove it, I believe that a few seconds after he had murdered Polly Nichols, Endacott was startled to see Charles Cross walking towards him. Thinking fast, he may have told Cross the truth and said that he was a policeman but was on special observational duty and for some reason or another it would not be good if he was to become involved in any murder inquiry. If Endacott was clever enough he could have persuaded the men to forget they had ever seen him. However, when Cross met PC Mizen in Hanbury Street, he was in such an agitated state he may have just blurted out the words without thinking, thus giving us a clue as to what really happened. Unfortunately, the discrepancies in the two statements were not questioned at the time so we shall never know exactly what was said before PC Mizen went to Buck's Row.

Shortly after Cross and Paul had left the murder scene 38-year-old PC John Neil discovered the body whilst walking from Baker's Row, eastwards towards Brady Street. He quickly summoned PC Thain, whose beat along Brady Street took about thirty minutes, by signalling with his lamp.

Polly Ann Nichols' body was lying across the road from Essex Wharf, a warehouse encompassing the Brown & Eagle wool warehouse and Schneider's Cap Factory. The body was in the gateway entrance to Brown's stable yard, which was situated between a board school to the west and terraced houses belonging to tradesmen to the east. It was almost underneath the window of Emma Green, a widow, who lived with her daughter and two sons in 'New Cottage', which was the first house next to the stable gates. On the night of the murder Mrs Green stated that one of her sons went to bed at 9.00 pm, the other following at 9.45 pm. Mrs Green and her daughter, who shared a first-floor room at the front of the house, retired at 11.00 pm. Although she said she was a light sleeper, Mrs Green heard nothing until she was woken by the police conducting their investigation. Opposite the murder site lived the manager of Essex Wharf, a Mr Walter Purkiss, with his wife and a servant. Purkiss and his wife retired to bed at 11.00 pm and 11.15 pm respectively. Both of them stated that they had had a restless night and Mrs Purkiss believed that she had been pacing the room at the time of the murder, but neither of them saw or heard anything out of the ordinary.

At the scene of the murder, PC Neil sent PC Thain to fetch Dr Rees Ralph Llewellyn, whose surgery was at 152 Whitechapel Road. Dr Llewellyn put the time of the call out at 4.00 am. PC Mizen arrived at the scene shortly after 4.15 am, having come from his encounter with Cross and Paul in Hanbury Street. PC Neil promptly sent him to fetch the ambulance.

Dr Llewellyn had meanwhile arrived at Buck's Row and began his examination of the woman. Sergeant Kerby, who had been in the row shortly before the murder, arrived at about the same time as the doctor. Dr Llewellyn made a cursory examination of the body and pronounced Polly dead. Mizen, who had been to Commercial Street Police Station for assistance and the ambulance (a hand-drawn cart), had also arrived back on the scene and Dr Llewellyn ordered that the body be taken west along Buck's Row to the mortuary shed at the back of the Old Montague Street workhouse. When Polly's body was lifted and placed on the ambulance Dr Llewellyn noticed that there was 'a wine glass and a half of blood in the gutter at her side', and he had no doubt that she had been killed where she lay.

Before the body was moved, three slaughtermen from Barber's Knacker's Yard in Winthrop Street arrived on the scene. They were Henry Tomkins, James Mumford, and Charles Brittain. Tomkins told the inquest that he had been told of the murder by PC Thain at 4.00 am. If this was true then Thain must have gone to the knacker's yard before going to fetch Dr Llewellyn. Thain claimed that the men were at the scene when he returned with the doctor. However, Thain's cape was found at the knacker's yard and whilst he denied ever having visited there, saying that he had sent his cape there with another officer, the inquest jury was more than likely right in thinking that he tended to stop there for a chat, when he should have been on his beat.

It is interesting to note that while Dr Llewellyn was examining the body, an unknown man walked along Buck's Row, passing the scene. A few moments later, Patrick Mulshaw, who lived at 3 Rupert Street in Whitehall and who was employed by the Whitechapel Board of Works as a nightwatchman in Winthrop Street, which runs parallel with Buck's Row, spoke to a man. At the inquest Mulshaw said that he had heard nothing during the night, but said, 'Another man then passed by, and said "Watchman, old man, I believe somebody is murdered down the street."'

The man that spoke to Mulshaw was probably the man who had just come down Buck's Row. What is strange about Mulshaw's statement are the words 'another man', meaning that someone else had passed him by as well. This is another aspect of the case I find very odd. Why didn't the police follow up and question Mulshaw about the statement he made? Could they have been hiding something?

PC Thain, Sergeant Kerby, and another officer from H Division, took the body to the mortuary while PC Neil stayed at the scene of the murder. At about 4.30 am, Inspector John Spratling, a 48-year-old officer with eighteen years' service, arrived at the scene to witness Mrs Green's son, James, cleaning the blood from the cobblestones. Following on from this incident, when evidence was probably removed from the scene of a crime before a proper examination was done, police standing orders were changed. In future, the officer finding the body was to stay with it – as Neil had done. The first assisting officer to arrive was to go for a doctor and any other officers were to go to a police station to report the find. An inspector was to then go to the site. The body and its surroundings should not be touched except as ordered by a doctor or the inspector.

Finding he could do nothing at the scene of the murder, Inspector Spratling went with PC Neil to the mortuary at 5.00 am. As the inspector was taking down details of the body to try and get a positive identification, the victim's skirt was lifted and serious abdominal mutilations were discovered. Inspector Spratling sent for Dr Llewellyn again.

Whilst the body was at the mortuary, Detective Sergeant Patrick Enright, a 39-year-old officer of fourteen years' service, was given temporary charge of it and he left instructions that the body was not to be touched until it had been fully examined. The mortuary attendants, Robert Mann and James Hatfield, disregarded these instructions. Mann and Hatfield were both paupers; Hatfield being an inmate of Whitechapel Workhouse. At the later inquest, a disagreement broke out as to exactly what they had been told to do with the body. Mann claimed that he had received no instructions to wash and lay out the body, but for some reason the coroner, Wynne Baxter, instructed the jury to disregard the evidence of Mann as he had fits and was somewhat unreliable. Hatfield denied having been told not to touch the body by D. S. Enright and was defended by the coroner, although he had already admitted that his memory was bad. Whatever the reason for the mix up, by the time Dr Llewellyn arrived to examine the body it had been cleaned and any possible evidence had been lost.

Back in Buck's Row, several spots of blood had been found a short distance from where the body had lain. However, it was later thought that these could have come from the clothing or the tools of the three slaughterhouse workmen as they came to view the body. There were also unconfirmed reports of drops of blood being

Elizabeth Cass arrested

Elizabeth Cass charged

Mrs Bowman

Mr Newton, the magistrate

Elizabeth Cass cautioned by Mr Newton

Elizabeth Cass

Cass and Bowden Endacott as seen by the newspapers

The hearing against Endacott

AN APPEAL FOR £250

to assist

POLICE CONSTABLE ENDACOTT

in his defence.

THE CHARGE AGAINST ENDACOTT.—Mrs. ELDRIDGE SPRATT, late Lady Adjutant of the Corps of Commissionaires, has undertaken, at the request of several ladies, to collect funds on behalf of Police Constable Endacott, who she says, takes the charge laid against him much to heart and states that he has done his duty. All the money he obtained from his comrades is expended, and as witnesses will have to be brought to London to meet the case, he is in much need of assistance. He has a wife and six children. If reverses should befall him Mrs. Spratt of 11, Hinde Street, Manchester Square, undertakes to do her best for the children. Any Subscriptions may be sent to the London & County Bank, Hanover Square, and its expenditure will be duly announced.—DAILY CHRONICLE.

The smallest Contributions will be thankfully received.

An appeal for funds for Endacott

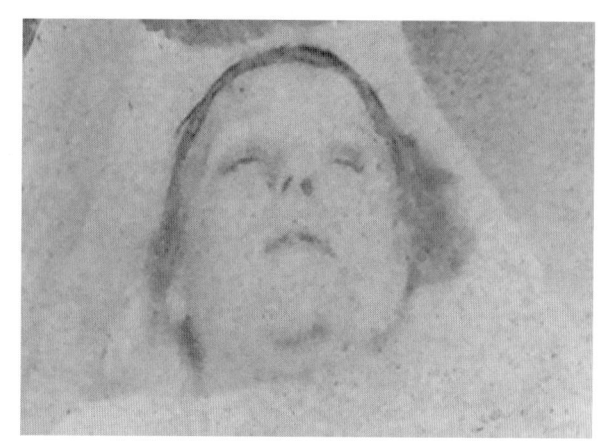

Mary Ann
'Polly' Nichols'
mortuary
photograph

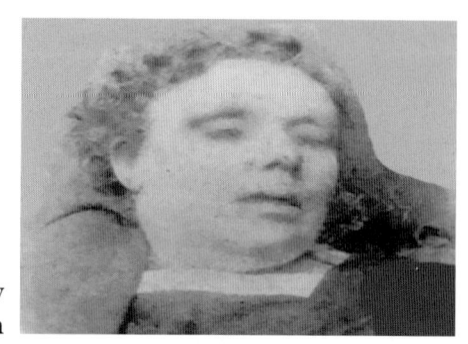

Annie Chapman mortuary
photograph

Annie Chapman and
her husband John

The backyard of 29 Hanbury Street where Annie Chapman's body was found

The passage at 29 Hanbury Street leading to the backyard

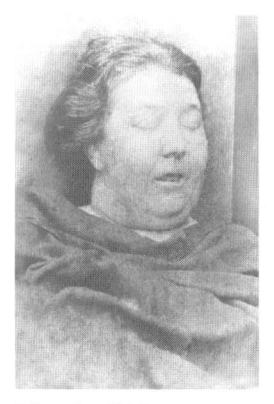

Martha Tabram mortuary photograph

Elizabeth Stride mortuary photograph

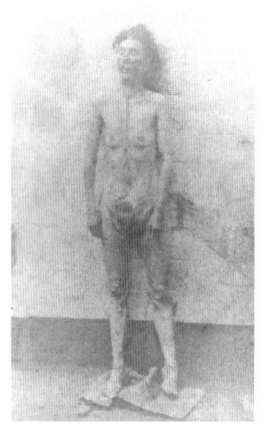

Catherine Eddowes
mortuary photograph

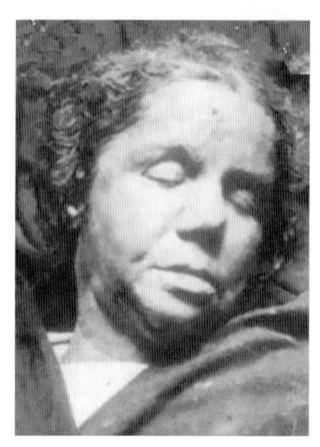

Alice McKenzie
mortuary photograph

Where Mary Kelly
was found murdered

Mary Kelly's room the day of
her murder

Mary Kelly crime scene

POLICE NOTICE.

TO THE OCCUPIER.

On the mornings of Friday, 31st August, Saturday 8th, and Sunday, 30th September, 1888, Women were murdered in or near Whitechapel, supposed by some one residing in the immediate neighbourhood. Should you know of any person to whom suspicion is attached, you are earnestly requested to communicate at once with the nearest Police Station.

Metropolitan Police Office,
30th September, 1888.

Notice issued by the police in 1888

Mitre Square where Catherine Eddowes was murdered. The murder site is now a flowerbed (*Author's Own*)

Buck's Row where Mary Ann Nichols was found. The murder site is now the pavement between the two cars (*Author's Own*)

The site of No 29 Hanbury Street today (*Author's Own*)

The former Wentworth Garden dwellings in Goulston Street, near to where Catherine Eddowes was found (*Author's Own*)

Henriques Street, which was formerly Berner Street, and the site of Elizabeth Stride's murder (*Author's Own*)

Mary Ann Nichols – Murdered 31 August 1888

seen in Brady Street and a Mrs Colwell, who lived there, claimed that during the night she heard a woman running and screaming 'Murder! Police!' No blood spots were found however, and the police dismissed the story.

At the mortuary the dead woman's clothes were searched and examined for any clues as to her identity. She was found to be wearing:

A black straw bonnet trimmed with velvet.

A reddish brown Ulster coat with several large brass buttons bearing the pattern of a woman on horseback accompanied by a man.

A brown Lindsey frock.

A white flannel chest cloth.

Blackribbed wool stockings.

Two petticoats, one grey wool, one flannel. Both were stencilled on the bands with 'Lambeth Workhouse'.

Brown stays (short).

Flannel drawers.

Men's elastic (spring) sided boots with the uppers cut and steel tips on the heels.

She had in her possession:

A comb.

White pocket handkerchief.

Broken piece of mirror (which was a prized possession in a lodging house).

The overall impression of the clothes was that they were shabby and stained.

After enquiries, Mary Ann Monk said she thought the body was of Mary Ann Nichols, whom she had known at Lambeth Workhouse. Ellen Holland later made a positive identification of her friend.

Dr Llewellyn made a detailed report of the injuries he found for the inquest. The report was printed in *The Times*:

> Five teeth were missing, and there was a slight laceration of the tongue. There was a bruise running along the lower part of the jaw on the right side of the face. That might have been caused by a blow from a fist or pressure from a thumb. There was a circular bruise on the left side of the face which also might have been inflicted by the pressure of the fingers. On the left side of the neck, about 1in. below the jaw, there was an incision about 4in. in length, and ran from a point immediately below the ear. On the same side, but an inch below, and commencing about 1in. in front of it, was a circular incision, which terminated at a point about 3in. below the right jaw. That incision completely

severed all the tissues down to the vertebrae. The large vessels of the neck on both sides were severed. The incision was about 8in. in length, the cuts must have been caused by a long-bladed knife, moderately sharp, and used with great violence. No blood was found on the breast, either of the body or the clothes. There were no injuries about the body until just about the lower part of the abdomen. Two or three inches from the left side was a wound running in a jagged manner. The wound was a very deep one, and the tissues were cut through. There were several incisions running across the abdomen. There were three or four similar cuts running downwards, on the right side, all of which had been caused by a knife which had been used violently and downwards. The injuries were from left to right and might have been done by a left handed person. All the injuries had been caused by the same instrument.

William Nichols, Polly's estranged husband, confirmed that it was her body when he arrived at the mortuary, respectfully dressed and carrying an umbrella, on the night of 1 September. He met Polly's father, Edward Walker, who had also come to see the body. With Edward was William's son, now a 23-year-old engineer. Edward said, 'Well, here is your son, you see. I have taken care of him and made a man of him.' William Nichols is said to have replied, 'Well I really did not know him; he has grown so and altered.' Edward John, William's son, never spoke to his father until after the funeral of his mother.

When he looked at the body of his wife William said, 'Seeing you as you are now, I forgive you for what you have done to me.' He came out of the mortuary room pale and visibly shaken, and said, 'Well, there is no mistake about it. It has come to a sad end at last.'

Mary Ann Nichols was buried at Little Ilford on 6 September 1888.

Shortly after the murder, the residents of Buck's Row applied to get the name of the Row changed. It is now called Durward Street.

POSTSCRIPT

The two men who first found the body of Polly Nichols, Charles Cross and Robert Paul, continued on their way to work after reporting the find to Constable Mizen. Cross was surprised when Paul suddenly disappeared into Corbetts Court as they reached the corner of Hanbury Street and Commercial Road. He did not realise that this was where he worked.

Mary Ann Nichols – Murdered 31 August 1888

Afterwards, whilst Paul made himself readily available to give interviews to the newspapers, it took the police a considerable time to find him. The inquest into Polly's death opened on 1 September, and Cross gave his evidence the following day. Paul did not come forward until two weeks later. It is not known why he was so reluctant, but it has been speculated that he may have been trying to conceal some ordinary crime that he didn't want investigating, or that he may have been afraid of one of the local gangs that terrorised the area. He could also have been threatened by Endacott to keep his mouth shut.

We shall never know the real reason, but during the two weeks the police were searching for him, another murder took place.

CHAPTER 6

The Search for the Ripper

Following the murder of Mary Ann Nichols, the police made extensive enquiries among the local prostitutes and were given details of a man who had been demanding money and menacing them if they didn't pay. This practice of blackmailing was very common in the area. It was also a common occurrence for the police to blackmail prostitutes. The man the prostitutes gave details to the police about was nicknamed Leather Apron.

On 5 September, *The Star* gave a full description of the man. He was described as a short, thickset man of 38-40 years old. He had black hair, a black moustache and was said to have an exceptionally thick neck. He usually wore a close-fitting cap and always wore a leather apron. The newspaper went on to say that he always carried a sharp knife and was always threatening the women with the words: 'I'll rip you up.' His movements were said to be silent and sinister and his eyes were said to glint. His smile was repulsive. *The Star* reporter who noted these observations had interviewed fifty women in the space of three hours and they all gave the same description. Leather Apron was also said to be a specialist slipper maker, and to have threatened women in other parts of London. The next description they gave became a primary feature in the rising fervour about his identity: they said he was Jewish, or at least of strongly Semitic appearance.

Jews whose ancestors had been admitted to the land by Oliver Cromwell had long settled in Whitechapel. Most of them were poor and sold second-hand clothes in the street markets. Charles Booth wrote in the year 1881:

> The newcomers have gradually replaced the English population in whole districts which were formerly outside the Jewish quarter. Formerly in Whitechapel, Commercial Street roughly dividing the Jewish haunts of Petticoat Lane and Goulston Street from the rougher English quarter lying in the east. Now the Jews have flowed across that line; Hanbury Street, Fashion Street, Pelham Street, Booth Street, Old Montague Street, and many streets and lanes and alleys have fallen before them; they

fill whole blocks of model dwellings; they have introduced new trades as well as new habits and they live and crowd together and work and meet their fate independent of the great stream of London life surging around them.

Racism was widespread amongst working-class people of Whitechapel who resented the foreigners coming over and taking jobs, when there was not enough work to go around amongst the English. It was also rife among the higher classes, as the following case of flagrant anti-foreign bias shows. The magistrate in question, a Mr Saunders, aroused widespread controversy after the following events were reported in the *East End News* on 14 September 1888:

> Mr Saunders, magistrate sitting at Worship Street, was strongly criticised for his attitude towards an applicant for summons on behalf of a Polish tailor, [it is believed that the tailor was Jewish] whose employer, it was asserted, owed him wages which he was unable to get after repeated application. 'Why doesn't the man speak for himself?' asked the magistrate. 'He is a native of Poland,' was the reply. 'Then let him go to Poland,' retorted the magistrate, adding however, on the applicant turning to leave the box, that he had better explain the matter. On the case being laid before him, the magistrate observed that the Pole had no business in this country, and that he was taking the bread out of the mouths of Englishmen. 'You may have your summons,' he added, 'but I hope you won't succeed.'

Even amongst the hierarchy of the Metropolitan Police, anti-Semitism was prevalent. On the day of Polly Nichols' murder, Dr (later Sir) Robert Anderson was appointed assistant commissioner for crime. He was convinced the murderer, who would later became known as Jack the Ripper, was a Polish Jew. When his memoir *The Lighter Side of My Official Life* was published he wrote, 'the only person who ever had a good look at the murderer at once identified him, but when he learned that the suspect was a fellow Jew he declined to swear to him.' The memoir was first published, in serialisation form, in *Blackwood's Magazine* in 1910. When the actual book was published, Anderson had made some changes and the above statement now read: 'I will merely add that the only person who ever had a good view of the murderer unhesitatingly identified the suspect the instant he was confronted with him, but refused to give evidence against him.' He then added: 'In saying that he was a Polish Jew I am merely stating definitely ascertained fact. And my words are meant to specify race, not religion. For it would outrage all religious sentiment to talk of the religion of a loathsome creature whose utterly unmentionable vices reduced him to a lower level than that of the brute.'

It is not known exactly why Anderson changed the wording of his memoir, but it is believed he was wary of possible libel action being taken against him with regards to other remarks he had made about a letter that had been received, supposedly from Jack the Ripper himself. Anderson was convinced a journalist who was trying to sell newspapers and keep the story of the outrages in the headlines penned the letter.

At the time of Polly Nichols' murder, the only suspect the police had was Leather Apron. He was said to hang around the Princess Alice public house in Commercial Street, and during the previous year had served a seven-day gaol sentence for assaulting a woman. He was also said to have a friend called Mickeldy Joe, whom he sometimes stayed with in a lodging house of Brick Lane. When a reporter from *The Star* went to the lodging house on 4 September, Joe was there. He and the other residents denied that they knew anyone called Leather Apron, and insisted he *certainly* did not live there. The reporter felt that Joe's presence in the house shall we say 'encouraged' the other residents to make this denial.

The police tried to dampen the rising tide of anti-Semitism by stating that there was 'only suspicion' against Leather Apron. On 7 September however, Inspector Joseph Henry Helson, of J Division, sent his weekly report into Scotland Yard. In it he stated:

> The inquiry has revealed the fact that a man named Jack Pizer, alias Leather Apron, has for some considerable period of time been in the habit of illusing [sic] prostitutes in this, and other parts of the Metropolis, and careful search has been and is continued to be made to find this man in order that his movements may be accounted for on the night in question, although at present there is no evidence whatever against him.

It is known that John Pizer was a Polish Jewish boot finisher who had probably been born in England. It is interesting to note that Helson's report gives Pizer's forename as Jack, thus intimating that Helson's informant must have been someone who knew Pizer extremely well, as all other reports about him give his name as John.

Pizer lived at 22 Mulberry Street although on the night of 30-31 August 1888, he was staying at Crosshinghams Lodging House. He said that he had had supper there at about 11.00 pm on the Thursday night and then went out to the Seven Sisters Road, where he saw the glow in the sky from the fire burning at the docks. According to his statement to the police, he arrived back at his lodging house at 1.30 am and spoke to the lodging house manager. He also said that he had spoken to a police constable whilst in Seven Sisters Road. His story was investigated and he was released.

The facts leading up to Pizer's arrest make interesting reading, especially as there are discrepancies in his alibi in the days following the murder of Polly Nichols. Pizer stated that the night after the murder he went to Westminster, where he stayed in a lodging house in Peter Street for a week. He said that he never left Westminster, but then he made a curious remark. He stated that on Sunday 2 September, he had been in Church Street when two unknown women asked him if he was the man the police were looking for; he took this to mean Nichols' murderer. However, if the Church Street he was in – which is today's Fournier Street, Spitalfields – it means that although he stated that he had spent the entire week in Westminster, he must, at some point have come back to the East End.

A crowd of people had gathered after the two women made it known that they suspected him, and a police officer from J Division is reported to have temporarily arrested him. Pizer was forced to flee the scene with the mob chasing him after the arresting officer refused to take him into custody. (The police denied that he was ever arrested on that day.) It is curious that the two women accused him of being Leather Apron on 2 September, when the story that the police were looking for him did not break in the press until two days later, on 4 September. It is more than likely that Pizer had tried to accost one of the two women and because of this they assumed that he must be the murderer.

On 6 September, Pizer went back home to Mulberry Street, where he stayed for four days. While he was there his brother warned him that there was 'a false suspicion against him'. Then on Monday, 10 September, Sergeant William Thick and another officer, both from H Division, went to 22 Mulberry Street. Pizer opened the door to them. When Thick said, 'You're just the man I want', Pizer is reported to have turned pale and trembled. Thick arrested Pizer and took him to Leman Road Police Station where he was placed in a number of identity parades.

The landlady of the Prince Albert public house in Brushfield Street, Spitalfields, was called to one of the identity parades because she had reported that a man had entered her pub with spots of blood on the back of his right hand. She was unable to identify Pizer. The following day, Sergeant Thick told *The Star* that he was 'almost positive' Pizer was Leather Apron. No other evidence was found against him however and after completing his statement he was released.

During the search for Leather Apron, the press were quick and eager to print any possible reference to him they could, as the following story from *The Times* on 10 September proves. It would seem that a young woman named Lyons met a strange man at 3.00 pm on 9 September in Flower and Dean Street. He asked her to come to the Queen's Head at 6.30 pm and have a drink with him. While they were in the pub the young woman noticed a large knife in the man's right-hand trouser pocket and called another woman's attention to the fact. The young woman was then startled to hear the man say: 'You are about the same style of woman as the one that's murdered.'

Miss Lyons replied: 'What do you know about her?'

The man replied, 'You are beginning to smell a rat. Foxes hunt geese, but they don't always find 'em.'

The man then hurried out the pub. Miss Lyons followed him until he reached Spitalfield Church, where he noticed that she was behind him. He rushed away so she could not follow any more. The interesting point about this story is that the newspaper's description of the man's appearance was in all material points identical to the published description of the man known as Leather Apron.

The previous day, while the search for Leather Apron was still going on, another murder had taken place – that of Annie Chapman, in Hanbury Street. On 11 September, the day he was released from Leman Street Police Station, Pizer was summoned to appear before the inquest into Annie's death to be cleared of any suspicion that he might be the culprit. In answer to the opening questions put to him, he stated that he was known as Leather Apron, and in his testimony, Sergeant Thick confirmed that he had 'known Pizer for many years, and when people in the neighbourhood spoke of Leather Apron they meant him.' There was still doubt though as to whether Pizer was in fact the Leather Apron that everyone had been referring to and the press were totally unable to confirm that he was. In a later interview, Pizer said that he had not known he was referred to as Leather Apron until Sergeant Thick arrested him, and Pizer's family and friends all strenuously denied that he was nicknamed as such. All later police reports, however, stated that John Pizer, known as Leather Apron, was an early suspect who had been cleared.

Pizer went on to take out libel actions against the newspapers that had so improvidently made statements about him, stating that 'the charges against me have quite broken my spirits, and I fear that I shall have to place myself under medical treatment.' It was reported that Pizer received handsome financial compensation from the newspapers and the sum of £5,000 was mentioned. The *East End Advertiser*, however, reported that this sum was seriously wide of the mark, and even £500 would be somewhat of an exaggeration. In one case it is known that he more than likely accepted £10 from Harry Dam, a reporter on *The Star*, on the assurance that he would not issue a libel writ against them. On 11 October 1888, a woman called Emily Patswold went up to Pizer, hit him and called him Leather Apron. Pizer took her to court where she was fined 10/- (50p).

In July 1897, Pizer died of gastroenteritis in the London Hospital. He was 47 years old and still resident in Mulberry Street.

CHAPTER 7

Annie Chapman – Murdered 8 September 1888

Annie Chapman was 47 years old when she died. She was born Eliza Anne Smith, in Paddington, in 1841. Her father, George Smith, was a Life Guardsman who married her mother, Ruth Chapman, in 1842. George and his family moved to Windsor in 1856 and in 1869 Annie met and married John Chapman at All Saints Church in Knightsbridge. John Chapman is described as a domestic head coachman; he is also believed to have been a relative of Annie's mother, Ruth, although the exact relationship is not known. In 1870 the couple were living in Bayswater and by 1873 they had moved to a mews off Berkeley Square, staying there until about 1881, when it is reported that John lost his post as a valet to a gentleman in Bond Street, because of Annie's dishonesty. They moved back to Windsor as John had found employment working for Joseph Weeks at St Leonard's Mill Farm Cottage. The couple stayed here for about twelve months. Annie and John had three children – two daughters, and one son. One of the daughters, Emily, died in 1882; the son was crippled, and it is believed he was sent to a cripple's institution.

Shortly before her daughter's death, Annie left the matrimonial home and went back to live in London. Allegedly her drunkenness and immorality broke up the marriage, but her friends described her as only occasionally drunk. Her husband, John, however, died in 1886 of cirrhosis of the liver and dropsy, so we cannot be sure of exactly who was to blame for the failure of the marriage. Up until the time of his death, John paid Annie 10/- (50p) allowance a week, albeit not always regularly. When John died, on Christmas Day, Annie, now finding herself with no income at all, lived by any means she could. She sold her own crochet work, matches or flowers, lived off men friends, and occasionally prostituted herself. At the time of John's death, she was living at 30 Dorset Street, with a sieve maker named, or nicknamed, Jack Sivvey. She had also been keeping company with a man called Edward Stanley, who later said that he had known Annie when she was living in Windsor. Stanley, who was also known as 'the pensioner', was a bricklayer, living at 1 Osborn Place, Brick Lane. He was known to some of his friends as an ex-soldier, who was drawing a pension from the Essex Regiment, although he later admitted that he had never been in, or drawn a pension from, any regiment. His only contact with the military being that he was in the Hampshire Militia.

From about May 1888, Annie was living mainly at Crossinghams Lodging House. Edward Stanley said that on many weekends he had paid for a bed for her.

The deputy, or manager, of Crossinghams was Timothy Donovan. Crossinghams was used by many of the characters involved in the murders of 1888, including Leather Apron. Donovan told the press that he knew Leather Apron by sight and had ejected him from the lodging house some time before the murders began, for threatening a woman. However, the police did not ask him to identify John Pizer after they had arrested him and it is believed that Donovan liked to make himself out to be a lot more important than he actually was. It is possible that Donovan was indicted of murdering his wife Mary in 1904, but there is no proof that this was the same Timothy Donovan who managed Crossinghams.

Sometime between 30 August and 6 September 1888, a fight broke out between Annie Chapman and a woman named Eliza Cooper. The fight, which was either started in The Britannia public house, or the kitchen at Crossinghams, or continued at one or the other, appears to have been about a florin (10p). It would seem that Annie told a man known as 'Harry the Hawker' that she had seen Eliza steal a florin from him and replace it with a halfpenny. Eliza stated that Annie then threw the halfpenny at her, in lieu of her soap that had been borrowed by Annie for Stanley's use. It would, however, appear that the main cause of the fight was rivalry over the favours being shared by both of them with regard to Harry the Hawker. Harry, probably wisely, kept well out of the way following the later events and although he was called as a witness at the inquest into Annie's death, he never actually appeared, as some members of the jury stated that they knew him and had no interest in hearing his testimony. Nothing else is really known about Harry and his story has disappeared from the pages of history. Annie suffered a black eye in the fight and bruising on her chest. The actual fight is not important in the chronology of Annie's last few days on Earth, but at the inquest it showed that the murderer did not cause those particular injuries.

At the inquest, Stanley stated that he had returned to Whitechapel on 1 September, after having been on duty with the 2nd Brigade Southern Division of the Hants Militia at Fort Elson in Gosport, where he had been since 6 August. He met Annie on the corner of Brushfield Street and they spent the Saturday and Sunday together. If his statement is correct, the fight must have taken place on 1 September, in the Britannia, as they were seen there on that day.

On Monday, 3 September, Amelia Palmer saw Annie in Dorset Street. Amelia, who lived at 30 Dorset Street with her husband Henry, was a friend of Annie's and knew her well. Amelia said that Annie had complained of feeling unwell and intended to go to her sister's in Vauxhall so she could get a pair of boots to enable her to go hop picking.

The next day, Amelia met Annie near Spitalfield Church. Annie again complained of feeling unwell – she said she'd had nothing to eat or drink that day – and said that she was going to the casual ward for a day or two. Amelia gave her 2d, warning her not to spend it on drink. The last time Amelia saw Annie alive was on Friday 7 September. She met her in Dorset Street and Amelia asked her if she was going to Stratford (a suburb of London), Annie said that she felt too ill to do anything, but added, 'it's no good my giving away. I must pull myself together and go out and get some money or I shall have no lodgings.' It is believed that Annie went to Stratford to prostitute herself.

It should be pointed out that in the report given at her inquest, H Division Police Surgeon Dr George Bagster Phillips said 'the deceased was far advanced in disease of the lungs and membranes of the brain, but they had nothing to do with the cause of death.' We can assume from Phillips' testimony, and how ill Annie was reported to be feeling, that she probably did not have much time to live, had she not been murdered.

The next time that Annie was seen after the encounter with Amelia Palmer was at Crossinghams, at about 11.30 pm on 7 September. Timothy Donovan said that Annie had asked him for permission to go and sit in the kitchen, which he allowed her to do. Donovan, though, told different stories concerning the events that occurred that day. On 10 September, *The Manchester Guardian* published a statement by Donovan saying that Annie had come to the lodging house at about 3.00 pm and asked to sit in the kitchen and he had not seen her again until about 1.45 am when he asked her for her 4d bed money. She said she had not got it so he turned her out. In another version of the story, we learn that she was allowed into the kitchen at 11.00 pm and left at 2.00 am. In yet a third version of the story, Donovan is supposed to have said that at 11.00 pm Annie passed the door of the lodging house and spoke to him. She had then returned at about 1.40 am, drunk and eating a baked potato. He asked her for her bed money and she is said to have replied, 'I haven't got it. I am weak and ill and have been in the infirmary.' As she left, she is reported to have said, 'Don't let the bed. I'll be back soon.'

It is thought that Donovan continually changed his story as an attempt to reduce the bad impression that many people had of him, and to make them think that he was not really the wicked landlord who turned an extremely sick woman out into the streets and into the arms of a murderer.

Whichever version is correct, it is known that at 12.12 am, she was seen in the kitchen at Crossinghams by William Stevens, a printer who lodged there. William said that he saw Annie pick up a piece of envelope that was beside the fireplace, put some pills in that had fallen from a broken pill-box, and leave the kitchen. The pills are probably some she received after going to the infirmary. Frederick Stevens, another lodger at Crossinghams, told *The Star* that he drank a pint of beer with Annie at 12.30 am. They probably went to the Britannia, arriving back at Crossinghams at about 1.30 am.

Whatever really happened we shall never know, the only certainty is that Annie was out on the street with nowhere to go. We can be sure that the last recorded words Annie was heard to speak were to John Evans, the elderly nightwatchman at Crossinghams. As she left, she told him that she had been to see her sister in Vauxhall and had just been out for a pint of beer. She also said that she did not have enough money for her bed, but would soon get it. Her last words were, 'I won't be long Brummy. See that Tim keeps the bed for me.' Evans said that he saw her go up Little Paternoster Row, in the direction of Brushfield Street. It was the last time she was seen alive.

Donovan, Stevens and Evans all described Annie as being drunk, yet Dr Phillips, who performed her post-mortem, stated that Annie's stomach had contained a little food, probably the baked potato, but no fluid. He was convinced that she had taken no strong alcohol for some hours previously. It is thought that the most Annie had to drink was a pint about three hours before she met her death and, as this was unlikely to get her drunk, we must assume that her appearance was due to serious illness, fatigue and physical deprivation.

The events of the next few hours are not known although there was a rumour that Annie had been seen drinking in The Ten Bells at about 5.00 am. The *East London Advertiser* reported that she was there until an ugly-faced man, wearing a skullcap, summoned her out. *The Manchester Guardian* attributed the story to 'the potman at The Ten Bells'. The police believed that the sighting was a case of mistaken identity.

Annie Chapman – Murdered 8 September 1888

The next probable sighting of Annie was at 5.30 am, when Elizabeth Darrell, or Durrell, described having seen a woman whom she identified as Annie on the pavement outside 29 Hanbury Street (the murder site). Mrs Darrell said that the man she was talking to was of a shabby genteel appearance, wearing a deerstalker hat and a dark coat. She estimated he was around 40 and had a dark complexion and foreign appearance – this usually meant Jewish. She said he was only a little taller than Annie, who was only a little over 5ft. Mrs Darrell said that she only saw him from the back. The man was heard to say, 'Will you?' Annie replied, 'Yes.' At around the same time, Albert Cadosch, a young carpenter living at 27 Hanbury Street, said that he went into the yard of his house and heard a voice coming from the yard of No 29, say 'No!'. After a few moments he heard something fall against the 5ft wooden fence dividing the yards. He though no more of it and went off on his way to work.

In 1888, Mrs Amelia Richardson occupied 29 Hanbury Street. Mrs Richardson, who had lived there for fifteen years, rented the first two floors and lived in the first-floor front room with her 14-year-old grandson, Thomas. She used the cellar and yard for her business of making packing cases. At work her son John and a man named John Tyler assisted her. Mrs Richardson sublet the rest of the house; it was the home for seventeen people.

Renting the ground floor was a Mrs Harriet Hardiman and her 16-year-old son. They used the ground-floor front room as a shop from which they sold cat's meat; the rear room was used as a kitchen to cook the meat and they both slept in the shop part of the house. A Mr Walker who lived there with his son rented the first-floor back room; Walker is described as feeble minded but very inoffensive. A Mr and Mrs Thompson and their adopted daughter occupied the second-floor front room. Thompson, who was a carman employed at Goodson's of Brick Lane, stated that he rose and went to work at 3.30 am, without going into the yard, and saw nothing unusual. Mr and Mrs Copsey, who described themselves as cigar makers, occupied the second-floor back room.

On the third-floor back room was a Sarah Cox, an elderly woman allowed to live there as a charity by Mrs Richardson; in the front room of the same floor lived John Davis. Davis had lived there with his wife and three sons for about two weeks prior to the murder. After a restless night, Davis, an elderly carman employed in Leadenhall Market, arose and made himself a cup of tea. At about 6.00 am he went into the yard and found the body of a woman, and later described his initial reaction: 'I saw a female lying down, her clothing up to her knees, and her face covered with blood. What was lying beside her I cannot describe – it was part of her body. I did not examine the woman; I was too frightened at the dreadful sight.'

Prior to Davis finding the body, at about 4.45 am, John Richardson, Amelia's son, had called at Hanbury Street to check the cellar door padlock whilst on his way to work because, as well as helping his mother, he also had a job as a porter at Spitalfields Market. He stated that he occasionally checked the building because a few months before someone had broken the padlock on the cellar door and stolen a hammer and saw. He also said that he had once found a prostitute and her client on the step and wanted to make sure the area was not being used for immoral purposes.

To help in understanding the general layout of the yard and passage, a brief description should now be given. The front of the building contained two doors, the right hand one leading into the shop and the other into a passageway off which led to stairs to the upper rooms. At the end of the passageway was a door that led into the rear yard. The doors leading from the street and the door into the yard were never locked due to the tenants coming and going at all hours of the day and night.

The door into the yard swung outwards from right to left and when open covered a small recess. As it was self-closing, Wynne Baxter, the coroner who presided over the inquest into Annie's death, described it as a swinging door. The yard itself was about four feet below the level of the passage and was reached by three stone steps. The position of the steps created a recess on their left that was about three feet from the fence that separated Nos 27 and 29 Hanbury Street. In this recess, Annie Chapman's body was found. She was lying on her back, the left side of her body parallel to the fence. Her dress was pulled up to her knees, exposing her striped stockings; and her intestines lay across her left shoulder.

There are two versions as to what John Davis did next. *The Times*, on 10 September, stated that Davis ran out into Hanbury Street and called in PC Pinnock, 238H, who sent information to the police station in Commercial Street. The other, most popular version, states that Davis went out into the street and called to James Green and James Kent, who worked at John & Thomas Bayley's Packing Case Manufacturers, at 23A Hanbury Street. According to Davis' inquest testimony, the two men entered the passage and looked at the body but did not go into the yard, then all three of them went to look for a police officer; Davis going directly to Commercial Street Police Station. It was reported that James Kent did not directly go and look for an officer, but went and got himself a brandy before obtaining a canvas to cover the body. There is another version of this story as well though. It would seem that the first senior officer at the site of the murder; 38-year-old Inspector Joseph Luniss Chandler, an officer of fifteen years' service, sent for Dr Bagster Phillips, then to Commercial Street for an ambulance, cleared the passageway of the crowd of onlookers who had appeared and then covered the body with sacking.

Dr Bagster Phillips, whose surgery was at 2 Spital Square in Spitalfields, was called out at 6.20 am and arrived at the murder scene ten minutes later. After examining the body and pronouncing Annie dead, he ordered that the body be taken to the mortuary in Old Montague Street. Before the body was moved, it was noted that the contents of Annie's pocket (which had been cut open) were lying in a tidy pile; there was a piece of muslin, two combs, and probably, two brightly polished farthings. It was noted that two brass rings Annie normally wore had been torn off her finger. The murderer may have thought that they were gold. The police also found the piece of torn envelope with the two pills that Annie had taken earlier. Another find that caused a sensation at the time, was of a folded and damp leather apron. Later, however, Mrs Richardson came forward and said that it was her son John's apron; she had washed it and left it in the yard to dry. When word of the apron circulated, and with the search for Leather Apron still on everyone's mind, anti-Semitic violence erupted on the streets. Gangs of men who proclaimed that 'no Englishmen would commit such murder' beat up Jews. What they tended to forget though was that no Jew would commit such a murder either. The letting of blood in such a way was completely abhorrent to an orthodox Jew.

After the body was taken to the mortuary, a mistake was made. The nurse on duty, Mary Simonds, was ordered by the clerk to the Parish Guardians to strip and wash the body; this she did with the help of a woman named Frances Wright. To say that Bagster Phillips was annoyed when he arrived to do the autopsy is an understatement. At the inquest he complained about the interference of the clerk in a police matter and about the terrible condition of the Old Montague Street mortuary. Wynne Baxter upheld his complaints.

When Annie's clothes and possessions were examined the following list was made:

Long black figured coat that came down to her knees.
Black skirt.
Brown bodice.
Another bodice.
Two petticoats.

Large pocket worn under the skirt and tied about the waist (empty when found).

Lace up boots.

Red and white striped stockings.

Neckerchief, white with a wide red border (folded tri corner and knotted at the front of her neck. She was wearing it thus when she leaves Crossinghams.)

Scrap of muslin.

One small toothcomb.

Scrap of envelope she had taken from the kitchen at Crossinghams that contained two pills.

Dr Phillips described the body as he found it in the yard and his statement was reported thus:

> The left arm was placed across the left breast. The legs were drawn up, the feet resting on the ground, and the knees turned outwards. The face was swollen and turned on the right side. The tongue protruded between the front teeth, but not beyond the lips. The tongue was evidently much swollen ... . The body was terribly mutilated ... the stiffness of the limbs was not marked, but was evidently commencing. ... the throat was dissevered deeply ... the incisions through the skin were jagged, and reached right round the neck... . On the wooden paling between the yard in question and the next, smears of blood, corresponding to where the head of the deceased lay, were to be seen. These were about 14 inches from the ground, and immediately above the part where the blood lay that had flowed from the neck. ... the instrument used at the throat and abdomen was the same. It must have been a very sharp knife with a thin narrow blade, and must have been at least 6in. to 8in. in length, probably longer. ... the injuries could not have been inflicted by a bayonet or sword-bayonet. They could have been done by such an instrument as a medical man used for post-mortem purposes, but the ordinary surgical cases might not contain such an instrument. Those used by slaughtermen, well ground down, might have caused them. ... the knives used by those in the leather trade would not be long enough in the blade. There were indications of anatomical knowledge which were only less indicated in consequence of haste. The whole of the body was not present, the absent portions being from the abdomen. The mode in which these portions were extracted showed some anatomical knowledge ... the deceased had been dead at least two hours, and probably more... . There was no evidence ... of a struggle having taken place. ... the deceased entered the yard alive... . A handkerchief was round the throat ... it was not tied on after the throat was cut.

Dr Baxter's post-mortem observations were also reported:

> He noticed the same protrusion of the tongue. There was a bruise over the right temple. On the upper eyelid there was a bruise, and there were two distinct bruises, each the size of a man's thumb, on the forepart of the top of the chest. The stiffness of the limbs was now well marked. There was a bruise over the middle part of the bone of the right hand. There was an old scar on the left of the frontal bone. The stiffness was more noticeable on the left side, especially in the fingers, which were partly closed. There was an abrasion over the ring finger, with distinct markings of a ring or rings. The throat had been severed as before described. The incisions into the skin indicated that they had been made from the left side of the neck. There were two distinctive clean cuts on the left side of the spine. They were parallel with each other and separated by about half an inch. The muscular structures appeared as though an attempt had been made to separate the bones of the neck. There were various other mutilations of the body, but he was of opinion that they occurred subsequent to the death of the woman, and to the large escape of blood from the division of the neck. From these injuries he was satisfied as to the cause of death. The cause of death was apparent from the injuries he had described. From these appearances he was of opinion that the breathing was interfered with previous to death [it would seem that she was strangled before her throat was cut] and that death arose from syncope, or failure of the heart's action in consequence of loss of blood caused by severance of the throat... .
>
> The deceased was far advanced in disease of the lungs and membranes of the brain, but they had nothing to do with the cause of death. The stomach contained a little food, but there was not any sign of fluid. There was no appearance of the deceased having taken alcohol, but there were signs of great deprivation and he should say she had been badly fed... . The injuries were certainly not self-inflicted. The bruises on the face were evidently recent, especially about the chin and the sides of the jaw, but the bruises in front of the chest and temple were of longer standing – probably of days. He was of the opinion that the person who cut the deceased's throat took hold of her by the chin, and then commenced the incision from left to right [bloodstains on the fence meant she was probably lying on the ground when this occurred]. He thought it was highly probable that a person could call out, but with regard to an idea that she might have been gagged he could only point to the swollen face and protruding tongue, both of which were signs of suffocation.

The rest of Dr Phillips' evidence was given in a courtroom with only men present. The press of the day refrained from a full report and the next part of the evidence given is combined from reports in *The Times* and *The Lancet*:

> The abdomen had been entirely laid open: the intestines, severed from their mesenteric attachments, had been lifted out of the body and placed on the shoulder of the corpse. Whilst from the pelvis, the uterus and its appendages with the upper portion of the vagina and the posterior two-thirds of the bladder, had been entirely removed. No trace of these parts could be found and the incisions were cleanly cut, avoiding the rectum, and dividing the vagina low enough to avoid injury to the cervix uteri. Obviously the work was that of an expert – of one, at least, who had such knowledge of anatomical or pathological examinations as to be enabled to secure the pelvic organs with one sweep of the knife, which must therefore have been at least five or six inches in length, probably more. The appearance of the cuts confirmed him in the opinion that the instrument, like the one which divided the neck, had been of a very sharp character. The mode in which the knife had been used seemed to indicate great anatomical knowledge.
>
> He though he himself could not have performed all the injuries he described, even without a struggle, under a quarter of an hour. If he had done it in a deliberate way such as would fall to the duties of a surgeon it would probably would have taken him the best part of half an hour.

Amelia Palmer subsequently identified the body of her friend Annie Chapman. Annie was laid to rest on 14 September 1888, at Manor Park, with members of her family in attendance.

POSTSCRIPT

During my three years of research into Bowden Endacott and his connection with the Whitechapel murders I have read many publications and articles. One of the publications, *The Illustrated Police News* carried the following article and I found it very puzzling, as no further mention was made of it. It should be assumed that the officers looking into the murders would have followed up a report such as this published in their own newspaper, but it would appear they did not. I have decided to print the whole of the article as I believe it goes some way to showing that the police already knew that Bowden Endacott was the murderer. It is dated 22 September 1888:

Annie Chapman – Murdered 8 September 1888

The following facts which have just come to hand may furnish a clue by which the Hanbury-street murderer may be traced. On the day of the murder (the 8th instant) a man was seen in the lavatory of the City News Room, Ludgate–circus–buildings, changing his clothes. He departed hurriedly, leaving behind him a pair of trousers, a shirt, and a pair of socks. Unfortunately, no one connected with the establishment saw the man, or he would certainly have been stopped and questioned as to why he was changing his clothes there and leaving the old ones behind. Mr Walker, the proprietor of the News Rooms, states that he did not hear of the occurrence until late in the afternoon, when his attention was called to the clothes in the lavatory. He did not at the time attach any importance to the fact, and the clothes were thrown into the dust box and placed outside, being carted away in the City Sewers' cart on the Monday. On the following Tuesday, however, he received a visit from a man who represented himself to be a police-officer and asked for the clothes which had been left there on the Saturday. Mr Walker replied that if he wanted them he would have to go to the Commissioners of the City Sewers, telling him at the same time what he had done with them. Two detectives called on Thursday, and had an interview with Mr Walker, and they succeeded in finding a man who saw the party changing his clothes in the lavatory, and he gave the police a description of him. He is described as a man of respectable appearance, about thirty years of age, and wearing a dark moustache; but the police are very reticent about the matter, and decline to give any information on the subject. They evidently attach some importance to the affair, as Mr Walker again received a visit from two detectives. The police are now trying to trace the clothes, as it is hoped they will furnish some clue to lead to the identity of the man whom they are searching for.

Let us now consider a few points from this article:
1. Assuming that this was indeed the murderer changing his clothes, it is obvious that he could not have been a poor man, as quite simply he probably wouldn't have possessed many shirts and trousers and could not afford to throw away an old set of clothes.
2. If the finding of the clothes was not reported to the police, how is it that 'a man who represented himself to be a police-officer', came and asked for the clothes? Unless of course it was police officer Bowden Endacott.
3. The description of the man fits Bowden Endacott.
4. Why should the police be reticent about giving information when they were after all the help they could get from the public?

It is such a pity that all the City Police records were destroyed during the bombing of London in the Second Word War. I think the truth lay within them.

CHAPTER 8

Elizabeth Stride – Murdered 30 September 1888

The *first* murder that occurred on 30 September was of Elizabeth Stride. I believe that her murderer was fortunate that he killed on the same night as Jack the Ripper took the life of Catherine Eddowes. Even though Elizabeth Stride is considered to be one of the canonical five, she was undoubtedly murdered by her boyfriend Michael Kidney. However, due to the slight similarity to the previous murders, and the general consensus that any murder in the Whitechapel area must be the work of the Ripper, the police came to the conclusion that he had been disturbed and had gone on to murder Catherine Eddowes in Mitre Square.

The reason I do not think that the Ripper murdered Elizabeth is that of location. The murderer of the other victims always chose an out-of-the-way spot to kill, Elizabeth Stride was murdered in Dutfield's Yard, Berner Street (now Henriques Street). The scene of the crime was also on the south side of Commercial Road, well away from the killer's usual sites on the north side of Aldgate High Street and Whitechapel Road. It was also continually in use at night with people coming from and going to the Worker's International Club that was situated on the right-hand side of the yard, and it is inconceivable that a man who had been so careful in his crimes should suddenly change his locality and take the risk of murdering where he knew there would be witnesses. The only person who would have taken her life would be an opportunist, someone whom Elizabeth knew and had been arguing with; maybe a fight that got out of hand.

Elizabeth Stride was 45 when she died and had been born in Torslanda near Gothenburg, Sweden. In 1865, at the age of 22, she was registered by the Gothenburg authorities as a prostitute and a year later she moved to London where she met and married John Thomas Stride, giving her address as 67 Gower Street. It is believed that she and John ran a coffee house in Upper North Street, Poplar, between 1870–2, and then at 178 Poplar High Street between 1872–4. The marriage seems to have been going through a bad patch by 1877 as Elizabeth was briefly admitted to Poplar Workhouse. By 1882 the marriage must have broken down completely, as Elizabeth started to live at 32 Flower and Dean Street, a common lodging house run by Elizabeth Tanner who stated that Elizabeth lived there off and on for the next six years, until the time of her death.

In 1885, Elizabeth was living with Michael Kidney, leaving him from time to time over the next three years. Kidney, who lived at 33 Dorset Street, was seven years younger than Elizabeth and they appear to have been continually at odds with each other. In April 1887, she had him charged with assault but failed to appear at the court to proceed with the prosecution. The day after Elizabeth's murder he went to Leman Street Police Station, drunk, and started berating the police about her murder and stating that he would have killed himself had he been the policeman on the beat where Elizabeth was murdered. Considering that he said he had not seen her for five days before her death and had not been upset by her absence, this seems an unusual statement to make. It's almost as though he was trying to prove it couldn't possibly have had anything to do with him.

On the day before her death, Elizabeth cleaned some rooms at her lodging house and Elizabeth Tanner paid her 6d. (2½p). At 6.30 pm that same evening she went for a drink at the Queen's Head, returning to the lodging house at 7.00 pm. Whilst she was there, she borrowed a clothes brush from Charles Preston, a barber and fellow resident, and gave Catherine Lane, who was a friend, a piece of velvet to look after until she returned. Lane said that Elizabeth had originally come to the lodging house because of an argument with Michael Kidney, although Kidney later denied this.

The next time Elizabeth was seen was at 11.00 pm when two labourers, J. Best and John Gardner, saw her leaving the Bricklayer's Arms in Settles Street with a man they described as about 5ft 5ins, with a black moustache, weak frame, sandy eyelashes and wearing a morning suit and a billycock hat. Best and Gardner said that the couple were sheltering from a rainstorm and the two labourers shouted out to Elizabeth, 'That's Leather Apron getting round you.'

Following on from this encounter Elizabeth was next seen at about 11.45 pm by William Marshall, a labourer who lived at 64 Berner Street. Marshall said that he saw her on the pavement opposite his house with a man he described as 5ft 6ins, of clerky appearance, stout, decently dressed in a black coat, dark trousers and a peaked sailor type cap. He was apparently English from his accent as Marshall heard him say, 'You would say anything but your prayers.' Marshall watched the couple walk up the road in the direction of Dutfield's Yard. From the general descriptions given by the three witnesses it is possible that Marshall saw the same man with Elizabeth as did Best and Gardner, however it would not have taken the pair of them forty-five minutes to walk from Settles Street to Berner Street, however slowly they ambled. The most obvious answer is that Elizabeth had finished with her previous client and had picked up another man somewhere along the way. If we assume that this was the case then Elizabeth must have had a busy evening for at 12.30 am, she was seen yet again, this time by PC William Smith, 452 H. Constable Smith said that he saw her standing in Berner Street, opposite Dutfield's Yard, talking to a man he described as 5ft 7ins, clean shaven, aged about 28, respectable looking and wearing dark clothes with a deerstalker felt hat.

The next, and most important of all the sightings of Elizabeth Stride and the man who was certainly her killer, took place at 12.45 am. Chief Inspector Swanson of the Metropolitan Police took down the following statement:

> 12.45 a.m. 30th Israel Schwartz of 22 Helen Street [sc. Ellen St], Backchurch Lane, stated that at this hour, on turning into Berner Street from Commercial Street [sc. Road] and having got as far as the gateway where the murder was committed, he saw a man stop and speak to a woman, who was standing in the gateway. The man tried to pull the woman into the street, but he turned her round and threw her down on the footway and the woman screamed three times, but not very loudly. On crossing to the opposite side of the street, he saw a second man standing lighting his pipe. The man who threw the woman down called out, apparently to the man on the opposite side of the road, 'Lipski', and then Schwartz walked away, but finding that he was followed by the second man, he ran so far as the railway arch, but the man did not follow so far.
>
> Schwartz cannot say whether the two men were together or known to each other. Upon being taken to the Mortuary Schwartz identified the body as that of the woman he had seen. He thus described the first man, who threw the woman down: – age, about 30; height 5ft 5in(s); comp., fair; hair, dark; small brown moustache, full face, broad shouldered; dress, dark jacket and trousers, black cap with peak, and nothing in his hands.
>
> Second man: age, 35; ht., 5ft 11in(s); comp., fresh; hair, light brown; dress, dark overcoat, old black hard felt hat, wide brim; had clay pipe in his hand.

The description of the first man matches the one seen with Catherine Eddowes in Mitre Square thirty to forty-five minutes later; however I am still of the opinion that they were two different men. An assailant with the indubitable prudence that he had shown during the previous murders would have taken into account the risk of killing a woman knowing that he had just been seen assaulting her, and whatever his state of mind his first thought would have been of escape. No, the truth of the matter is that probably Michael Kidney and his friend had been drinking in the Bee Hive public house that stood on the corner of Berner Street and Fairclough Street, only a matter of yards from the entrance to Dutfield's Yard. One of them had seen Elizabeth standing there; Michael Kidney came out and asked her where she had been for the past five days and wanted to know what she was doing. Jumping to the obvious conclusion that she was prostituting herself, he became angry and threw her to the ground. His friend, noticing Schwartz, shouted out the warning, 'Lipski', a term used as an anti-Semitic insult to Jews after the trial the previous year of Israel Lipski who murdered his fellow lodger Miriam Angel. Schwartz was of a strongly Semitic appearance.

To give credence to my theory I would like to quote from an article that appeared in *The Star* on 1 October. The paper interviewed Israel Schwartz and he recanted the following story, which was slightly, but tellingly, different from that he told to the police. Remembering of course that newspapers even then tended to embellish a story to sell more copies:

> Information which may be important was given to the Leman Street police yesterday by an Hungarian concerning this murder. The foreigner was well dressed, and had the appearance of being in the theatrical line. He could not speak a word of English, but came to the police station accompanied by a friend, who acted as interpreter. He gave his name and address, but the police have not disclosed them. A *Star* man, however, got wind of his call, and ran him to earth in Backchurch Lane. The reporter's Hungarian was quite as imperfect as the foreigner's English, but an interpreter was at hand, and the man's story was retold just as he had given it to the police. It is, in fact, to the effect that he saw the whole thing.
>
> It seems that he had gone out for the day ... . As he turned the corner from Commercial Road he noticed some distance in front of him a man walking as if partially intoxicated. He walked on behind him, and presently he noticed a woman standing in the entrance to the alleyway where the body was found. The half-tipsy man halted and spoke to her. The Hungarian saw

him put his hand on her shoulder and push her back into the passage, but feeling rather timid of getting mixed up in quarrels, he crossed to the other side of the street. Before he had gone many yards, however, he heard the sound of a quarrel, and turned back to learn what was the matter, but just as he stepped from the kerb a second man came out of the doorway of a public house a few doors off, and shouting out some sort of warning to the man who was with the woman, rushed forward as if to attack the intruder. The Hungarian states positively that he saw a knife in the second man's hand, but he waited to see no more. He fled incontinently to his new lodgings.

He described the man with the woman as about 30 years of age, rather stoutly built, and wearing a brown moustache. He was dressed respectably in dark clothes and felt hat. The man who came at him with a knife he also describes, but not in details. He says he was taller than the other but not so stout, and that his moustaches were red. Both men seemed to belong to the same grade of society. The police have arrested one man answering the description the Hungarian furnishes. The prisoner has not been charged, but is held for inquiries to be made. The truth of the man's statement is not wholly accepted.

It is interesting that the knife had changed from the pipe as reported by Swanson. Whatever the discrepancies, either man could have killed Elizabeth Stride.

The only thing we can say for sure is that her body was found at about 1.00 pm in Dutfield's Yard. There are two versions as to who exactly found the body. The first of these appeared in *The Weekly Herald*:

About five minutes to one o'clock on Sunday morning a youth, about twenty years of age, named Joseph Koster, was accosted by a little boy, who came running up to him as he was passing, on the opposite side, 40 Berner Street, used by the International Socialist Club, and told him that a woman was lying in the gateway next to the club with her throat cut. Koster immediately ran across the road, and saw a woman lying on her side in the gateway leading into Dutfield's stabling and van premises. The gate, which is a large wooden one, was partly opened, and the woman was lying partly in the street. He immediately rouses the neighbours, and, by the aid of a candle, it was seen that the woman's throat was cut open very nearly from one ear to another, and her lips were drawn up as if she had suffered sharp pain. She was dressed in black, and appeared to be in mourning. She wore a black bonnet, elastic-sided boots, and dark stockings. In her breast was a small bouquet of flowers, and in her left hand she held a small packet of scented cachous.

Constable Lamb, 252 East Division, soon afterwards appeared, and, with the assistance of two other constables, had the body, which was quite warm when found, removed to 40 Berner Street, where it was placed in a back room. To all appearances the woman seems to have been treated like the former victims, carried out and laid openly in the street. The case, in fact, resembles in many points the Buck's Row tragedy. The victim appears to have been about 23 years of age and it is not thought that she belonged to the locality in which she was found. The wound must have been inflicted with a very sharp instrument, no trace of which has yet been found, as it is very deep, and she was lying in a pool of blood, with which her clothes were saturated. The news of the tragedy spread with great rapidity, and a large number of Detectives from Scotland Yard, together with superintendents and inspectors of police, were soon on the spot. All those who were near the place at the time were detained, taken into the house, and closely examined as to the discovery, but nothing has yet been obtained which can afford a clue to the murder, and the police, having nothing whatever to go on, seem completely at their wits end ... Dr Blackhall and his assistant both examined the corpse, and declared that the woman must have been murdered, as she could not have taken her own life. Dr Phillips, who examined the woman in Hanbury Street was also called in, and made an examination of the woman; but he has been asked to keep the result a secret at present.

The second, and most widely accepted, version of events is that a man named Louis Diemschütz, a steward at the International Workingmen's Educational Club, returned to the gateway of the club at 1.00 am, driving his pony and cart. The entrance was very badly lit and the pony, upon turning into the gateway, pulled to the left and refused to go on. Diemschütz felt around with his whip and found the body of a woman lying in the gateway. He went into the club to report the find and returned to the scene with Morris Eagle and Issacs Kozebrodsky, two other members of the club. The police were called to the scene and the body was eventually taken to the mortuary.

Upon examining and stripping the body, Elizabeth Stride was found to be wearing:

Long black cloth jacket, fur trimmed around the bottom with a red rose and white maidenhair fern pinned to it. (She was not wearing the flower when she left the lodging house.)
Black skirt.
Black crepe bonnet.
Checked neck scarf knotted on left side.

Elizabeth Stride – Murdered 30 September 1888

Dark brown velveteen bodice.
Two light serge petticoats.
One white chemise.
White stockings (it is interesting that *The Weekly Herald* described her stockings as dark).
Spring sided boots.
Two handkerchiefs (one, the larger, is noticed at the post-mortem to have fruit stains on it).
A thimble.
A piece of wool around a card.
In the pocket in Elizabeth's underskirt are found:
A key (as of a padlock).
A small piece of lead pencil.
Six large and one small buttons.
A comb.
A broken piece of comb.
A metal spoon.
A hook (as from a dress).
A piece of muslin.
One or two small pieces of paper.
She is also found to be clutching a packet of cachous, which were used by smokers to sweeten the breath.
Dr Phillips performed the post-mortem and his report is as follows:

> The body was lying on the near side, with the face turned toward the wall, the head up the yard and the feet toward the street. The left arm was extended and there was a packet of cachous in the left hand ... the right arm was over the belly. The back of the hand and the wrist had on it clotted blood. The legs were drawn up with the feet close to the wall. The body and face were warm and the hand cold. The legs were quite warm. Deceased had a silk handkerchief round her neck, and it appeared to be slightly torn. I have since ascertained it was cut. This corresponded with the right angle of the jaw. The throat was deeply gashed, and there was an abrasion of the skin about 1½in. in diameter, apparently stained with blood, under her right brow. At 3 p.m. on Monday at St George's Mortuary ... Dr Blackwell and I made a post–mortem examination... . Rigor mortis was still thoroughly marked. There was mud on the left side of the face and it was matted in the head ... the body was fairly nourished. Over both shoulders, especially the right, and under the collar-bone and in front of the chest there was a bluish discoloration, which I have watched and have seen on two occasions since. There was a clean-cut incision on the neck. It was 6in. in length

and commenced 2½in. in a straight line below the angle of the jaw, ½in. over an undivided muscle, and then becoming deeper, dividing the sheath. The cut was very clean and deviated a little downwards. The artery and other vessels contained in the sheath were all cut through. The cut through the tissues on the right side was more superficial, and tailed off to about 2in. below the right angle of the jaw. The deep vessels on that side were uninjured. From this it was evident that the haemorrhage was caused through the partial severance of the left carotid artery. Decomposition had commenced in the skin. Dark brown spots were on the anterior surface of the left chin. There was a deformity in the bones of the right leg, which was not straight, but bowed forwards. There was no recent external injury save to the neck. The body being washed more thoroughly I could see some healing sores. The lobe of the left ear was torn as if from the removal or wearing through of an earring, but it was thoroughly healed. On removing the scalp there was no sign of bruising or extravasation of blood ... the heart was small, the left ventricle firmly contracted, and the right slightly so. There was no clot in the pulmonary artery, but the right ventricle was full of dark clot, the left was firmly contracted so as to be absolutely empty. The stomach was large, and the mucous membrane only congested. It contained partly digested food, apparently consisting of cheese, potato and farinaceous powder. All the teeth on the left lower jaw were absent... . The cause of death is undoubtedly from the loss of blood from the left carotid artery and the division of the windpipe. The blood had run down the waterway to within a few inches of the side entrance of the club. Roughly estimating it I should say there was an unusual flow of blood considering the stature and nourishment of the body.

Dr Phillips continued his report two days later on 5 October, and answered further questions from coroner Wynne Baxter thus:

He had made a re-examination with regard to the missing palate, and from very careful examination of the roof of the mouth he found that there was no injury to either the hard or soft palate. He had also carefully examined the handkerchiefs, and had come to the conclusion that the stains on the larger handkerchief were those of fruit. He was convinced that the deceased had not swallowed the skin or inside of a grape within many hours of her death. The apparent abrasion which was found on washing the flesh was not an abrasion at all, as the skin was entire underneath... . He found that the deceased was seized by the shoulders, pressed on the ground, and that the perpetrator of the deed was on the left side when he inflicted the wound. He was of the opinion that the cut was made from left to right of the deceased and from that, therefore, arose the unlikelihood of such a long knife having inflicted the wound described in the neck. The knife was not sharp pointed; but round and an inch across. There was nothing in the cut to show an incision of the point of any weapon... .

He could not form any account of how the deceased's right hand had become covered with blood. It was a mystery. He was taking it as a fact that the hand always remained in the position he found it in resting across her body. Deceased must have been alive within an hour of his seeing her. The injuries would only take a few seconds to inflict; it might have been done in two seconds. He could not say with certainty whether the sweets being found in her hand indicated that the deed had been done suddenly... . There was a great dissimilarity between this case and Chapman's. In the latter the neck was severed all round down to the vertebral column, the vertebral bone being enlarged with two sharp cuts, and there being an evident attempt to separate the bones... . The murderer would not necessarily be bloodstained, for the commencement of the wound and the injury to the vessels would be away from him, and the stream of blood, for stream it would be, would be directed away from him, and towards the waterway already mentioned... . He had reason to believe that the deceased was lying on the ground when the wound was inflicted.

The reference to grapes not being eaten referred to a claim a day earlier by Matthew Packer, a fruiterer, who lived at 44 Berner Street, and who sold fruit from his front room window with his wife. He told the police that he had seen nobody in the street when he closed the shutters on his shop at 12.30 am. When a report appeared in *The Evening News* on 4 October, stating that Packer had told two private detectives Grand and Batchelor – who had been hired by the Whitechapel Vigilance Committee and some newspapers to investigate the murders – that he had sold some grapes to Elizabeth Stride and a man an hour or more before her death, the police were naturally surprised. The private detectives had learned that a Miss Eva Harstein, who lived at 14 Berner Street, and her sister, Mrs Rosenfield, had seen a bloodstained grapestalk and some flower petals in the entry to Dutfield's Yard before the police washed the blood away. On 2 October, Grand and Batchelor found a grapestalk that had been swept into some rubbish. They then took Packer to the Golden Lane Mortuary to examine the body of Catherine Eddowes, to test his truthfulness, without revealing that it was the Mitre Square victim and not the woman found in Berner Street. Packer said that he had never seen the woman before. *The Evening News* sent a reporter out to visit him and printed his answer in bold capitals:

Except for a gentleman who is a private detective. NO DETECTIVE OR POLICEMAN HAS EVER ASKED ME A SINGLE QUESTION NOR COME NEAR MY SHOP TO FIND OUT IF I KNEW ANYTHING ABOUT THE GRAPES THE MURDERED WOMAN HAD BEEN EATING BEFORE HER THROAT WAS CUT!!!

The same day as the report appeared in the newspaper, Grand and Batchelor took Packer to St George-in-the-East Mortuary, where he had no hesitation in identifying Elizabeth Stride as the woman he had seen. On their return, the two private detectives found Sergeant White awaiting them. He had been sent to re-interview Packer, who told him, 'I believe she bought some grapes at my shop about twelve o'clock on Saturday.' Following on from this Grand and Batchelor took Packer to Scotland Yard to see Sir Charles Warren, who took down the following statement from Packer in his own hand:

Matthew Packer
Keeps a small shop in Berner Str has a few grapes in window. Black & white. On Sat night about 11 p.m. a young man from 25-30 – about 5.7. with long black coat buttoned up – soft felt hat, kind of [yankee?] hat – rather broad shoulders – rather quick in speaking. Rough voice. I sold him ½ pound black grapes 3d. A woman came up with him from Back Church end she was dressed in black frock and jacket a black crape bonnet, she was playing with a flower like a geranium white outside and red inside. I identify the woman at the St George's mortuary as the one I saw that night. – They passed by as though they were going up Com Road, but instead of going up they crossed to the other side of the road to the Board School, & were there for about ½ an hour till I shd. Say 11.30, talking to one another. I then shut up my shutters. After they passed over opposite to my shop, they went near to the Club for a few minutes apparently listening to the music. I saw no more of them after I shut up my shutters.
I put the man down as a young clerk.
He had a frock coat on – no gloves.
He was about 1½ inch or 2 or 3 inch – a little bit higher than she was.

Whilst the police believed Packer's statement was important, they were quick to refute the attack on them by *The Evening News* by saying that Packer contradicted himself and was unreliable. They also said that there was no evidence that Elizabeth Stride had eaten any grapes prior to her death and Packer was never called at the inquest to say that he had sold any grapes to her. The police also contradicted press reports that said some witnesses had seen a grape stalk clutched in her hand that dropped on the ground when the body was moved, confirming Eva Harstein's story. There was, however, confirmation that the police did find spat-out grape skins and seeds in the yard. This came about in 1938, when Chief Inspector Walter Dew, a detective constable in H Division at the time of the murders, published his memoir, *I Caught Crippen*. Why the police chose to ignore the fact that Elizabeth Stride was seen with a man just a short time before she died, and who could have been her murderer, is unknown.

Whilst many of the senior police officers on the case at the time were convinced that the murderer had been disturbed by Louis Diemschütz before he had chance to mutilate the body, Walter Dew remarked in his book that he always suspected that Stride was not one of the Ripper's victims.

Elizabeth Stride was buried in a pauper's grave no. 15509, in a cemetery in East London.

CHAPTER 9

Catherine Eddowes – Murdered 30 September 1888

Catherine Eddowes was a very foolish woman on the night she died. I believe that she went to see the man she suspected of being the murderer and probably tried to blackmail him. He, having no other choice, killed her.

Mitre Square, the scene of the murder, is today a pleasant area to walk through, albeit surrounded by office blocks. On the spot where Catherine's body was found now stands a bench in front of a flowerbed. In 1888, however, it was very different – a dark inhospitable place full of warehouses and the site of a former church called St James, which was demolished in 1874. At the north-west side of the square stood a warehouse belonging to Kearley & Tonge. Next to the warehouse, at number 3 Mitre Square, stood the house of PC Richard Pearse, 922 City. The spot where the murder took place could be seen clearly from his bedroom window.

The square is entered from the south west by means of Mitre Street. In 1888, on the right-hand side of the entrance stood three vacant houses forming a blind corner; Catherine's body was in front of one of the houses.

Catherine Eddowes was born on 14 April 1842 in Grasley Green, an area in Wolverhampton. At the time of her death she was 5ft, with hazel eyes and dark auburn hair. Unlike the other victims, there is no direct evidence that she was a prostitute and none of her acquaintances claimed to know she was a working girl; the only evidence we have is that she was seen talking to a strange man in the Duke's Street entrance to Church Passage, a covered entry that led into Mitre Square, on the night she was murdered. I believe this man was Bowden Endacott and that she had arranged to meet him there after going to see him following her release from Bishopsgate Police Station.

Before she was two years old, Catherine's father, George, moved his family from Wolverhampton to Bermondsey in London. Catherine stayed in London until the death of both her parents, within months of each other in 1851, then went back to Wolverhampton to stay in the care of an aunt. By the age of 21, she had met a man named Thomas Conway who was an army pensioner and they set up home together. Conway made a living by writing and selling chapbooks; these small pamphlets usually contained tales, ballads etc., and they sold them in and around Birmingham. During the time they were together, three children were born, Annie in 1865; George in 1868; and another son who was born between 1873 and 1875. By the time they separated in 1880, it appears they had moved back to London with Catherine having custody of Annie and Thomas having the two boys living with him.

In 1881, Catherine met John Kelly and moved in with him to Cooney's Lodging House, 55 Flower and Dean Street, living together as common-law husband and wife. Seven years later, when Catherine was murdered, they were still together. Kelly worked as a jobber around the markets, but his usual employment was with a fruit salesman named Lander.

In September 1888, they decided to go hop picking in Kent, but things did not go very well and they only stayed a few weeks. 'We didn't get along too well and started to hoof it home,' Kelly said later. They walked back to London with another couple, Emily Birrell, and her common-law husband. As they parted, the Birrells heading towards Cheltenham, Emily gave Catherine a pawn ticket, saying, 'I've got a pawn ticket for a flannel shirt. I wish you'd take it since you're going up to town. It is only for 2d, and it may fit your old man.' (After her death, Kelly heard that this ticket had been found on the body, and realised that it must be his wife.) Catherine took it and she and Kelly reached London on 27 September, and spent that night at the casual ward at Shoe Lane, separating the next morning. John went to 52 Flower and Dean Street to stay, and Catherine went to the casual ward at Mile End. While she was at the Shoe Lane casual ward, Catherine is reported to have said to the superintendent, 'I have come back to earn the reward offered for the apprehension of the Whitechapel murderer. I think I know him.' The superintendent is said to have warned her to be careful that he did not murder her. 'Oh, no fear of that,' she is said to have replied.

On 29 September, both Catherine and John were back at Cooney's Lodging House as Catherine had been turned out of the casual ward for some unknown reason. Being broke they decided to pawn a pair of John's boots at a pawnshop in Church Street and received 2/6d (12½p). The couple bought tea, sugar, and food, but by the afternoon they were both broke again. At the time, 2/6d would have brought quite a lot of food and beverages so we can safely assume that they must have spent some of the money on alcohol.

Catherine Eddowes – Murdered 30 September 1888

At 2.00 pm, the couple separated while in Houndsditch and Catherine said that she was going to Bermondsey to borrow some money from her daughter Annie, and would be back by 4.00 pm. Annie had married a man named Louis Phillips some time around 1885 and because of her mother's continual drinking and scrounging, she and Catherine had separated on bad terms with Annie and her husband spending the next few years moving around London to escape her mother's continuous borrowing. At the time of the disagreement, Annie was living in King Street, but had since moved leaving no forwarding address, so it is unlikely that Catherine would have been able to find her that afternoon. Annie later said that it had been twenty-five months since she last saw her mother and she did not see her on that day.

It is not known what Catherine did from 2.00 pm until she was next seen drunk at 8.30 pm. We can only assume that unless she met someone, who did not come forward after she died, and borrowed some money from them she must have prostituted herself. Whatever the reason, at 8.30 pm PC Louis Robinson, 931 City, was called to 29 Aldgate High Street where a drunken woman was doing an impression of a fire engine and causing a disturbance. When he arrived on the scene the woman finished the fire engine impression and proceeded to lie down on the pavement and fall asleep. With the assistance of PC George Simmons, also of the City Police, they stood her up and took her to Bishopsgate Police Station, arriving there at 8.45 pm. Sergeant James George Byfield was on duty at the time and when he asked Catherine her name she replied 'Nothing', so Sergeant Byfield locked her into a cell to sleep it off. At 9.45 pm, PC George Hutt, 968 City, came on duty and took charge of the prisoners in the cells, checking on them every half an hour during the next few hours.

At 12.15 am, Catherine was heard singing to herself in the cell and fifteen minutes later she called to PC Hutt asking when she would be released. 'When you are capable of taking care of yourself,' he replied. 'I can do that now,' she said.

At 12.55 am, Sergeant Byfield instructed PC Hutt to see if any of the prisoners was fit to be released and Catherine was found to be sober. Giving her name as Mary Ann Kelly and her address as 6 Fashion Street, she was released. As she left the station, she asked Hutt what the time was.

'Too late for you to get anything to drink,' he said.

'I shall get a damn fine hiding when I get home,' she replied.

'And serve you right. You had no right to get drunk.'

As she left Hutt noticed that she turned left, which took her in the opposite direction of what would have been the fastest way back to Flower and Dean Street. Catherine was now headed towards Aldgate High Street where she had got drunk, and her route would have taken her past the entrance to Duke Street, at the end of which was Church Passage that led to Mitre Square.

From the police station it takes about ten minutes to walk to Mitre Square; this leaves a thirty-minute gap until the time she is next seen. I believe that during this time Catherine contacted Bowden Endacott, whom she knew was on special duty patrolling the streets looking for the murderer. She then arranged to meet him in the Duke's Street entrance to Church Passage, as this was a quiet out-of-the-way place where she knew they would not be disturbed. They were, however, seen talking by three men who had just left the Imperial Club, in Duke's Street, at about 1.30 am. The men – Joseph Lawende, Joseph Hyam Levy and Harry Harris – all saw her conversing amicably with a man, and said that she had her hand upon his chest. The man was described as aged 30, with a fair complexion, brown moustache, salt and pepper coat, red neckerchief and sailor-style grey peaked cloth cap. There is a picture in existence of police officers 'in disguise'; some of them fit the description perfectly. The physical description also fits Bowden Endacott; apart that is from the age. At the time of the murders Endacott was 36, but I am not so sure that in a dimly lit alleyway anyone could judge a person's age with any great accuracy.

Approximately ten minutes after the three men had left the scene, PC James Harvey, 964 City, walked along Duke's Street and into Church Passage. He never entered Mitre Square and said that he saw nothing unusual. Five minutes later, PC Edward Watkins, who had been in the square only fifteen minutes earlier, entered it again from the opposite side to PC Harvey and found the body of Catherine Eddowes. Constable Watkins then went to the warehouse of Kearley & Tonge where he called to the nightwatchman, a retired police officer named George Morris. The first time Morris knew anything was wrong was when he heard Constable Watkins say, 'For God's sake, mate, come to assist me.' Morris asked what was the matter and Watkins replied, 'Oh dear, here's another woman cut up to pieces.' Morris picked up his lantern, went to see the body, and then ran into Aldgate where he found PC Holland, 814 City. Constable Watkins stayed by the body until Holland arrived and then sent him to fetch Dr George Sequeira, whose surgery was at 34 Jewry Lane. Dr Sequeira timed his arrival at Mitre Square at 1.45 am so taking that Constable Harvey had walked down Church Passage, from which the murder site could be easily seen, at 1.40 am and saw nothing, we must assume that the murderer had probably only about five minutes in which to commit the crime and inflict the injuries to Catherine's body.

Station Inspector Edward Collard, of Bishopsgate Police Station, was informed of the murder at 1.55 am and he sent for the City Police Surgeon, Dr Frederick Gordon Brown, before going to the murder scene, which he reached at 2.03 am. Superintendent McWilliam, Sergeant Foster, and Sergeant Jones followed him from Bishopsgate a few moments later. Sergeant Jones found three boot buttons, a thimble and a mustard tin containing the pawn tickets for Emily Birrell's man's shirt, and John Kelly's boots.

The body was transferred to Golden Lane Mortuary where Dr Brown examined it and made his report. The official police listing of Catherine's clothes and possessions, was as follows:

Black straw bonnet trimmed with green and black velvet and black beads, black strings.

Black cloth jacket, imitation fur edging round collar, fur round sleeves ... two outside pockets, trimmed black silk braid and imitation fur.

Chintz Skirt, three flounces, brown button on waistband. (The skirt was later described as having a pattern of chrysanthemums or michaelmas daisies and lilies).

Brown linsey dress bodice, black velvet collar, brown metal buttons down front.

Grey stuff petticoat, white waistband.

Very old alpaca skirt.

Very old ragged blue skirt, red flounce, light twill lining.

White calico chemise.

Man's white vest, button to match down front, two outside pockets.

No drawers or stays.

Pair of men's lace-up boots, mohair laces. Right boot has been repaired with red thread.

One piece of red gauze silk ... found on neck.

One large white handkerchief.

Two unbleached calico pockets.

One blue strip bed ticking pocket, waistband, and strings.

One white cotton handkerchief, red and white bird's eye border.

One pair brown ribbed stockings, feet mended with white.

Twelve pieces of white rag, some slightly bloodstained.

One piece of white coarse linen.

One piece of blue and white shirting (three cornered).

Two small blue bed ticking bags.

Two short clay pipes (black).
One tin containing tea.
One tin containing sugar.
One piece of flannel and six pieces of soap.
One small toothcomb.
One white handle table knife and one metal teaspoon.
One red leather cigarette case with white metal fittings.
One tin match box, empty.
One piece of red flannel containing pins and needles.
One ball of hemp.

Later reports in the press also added a pair of spectacles and one mitten to the list.

At 2.55 am, PC Alfred Long passed the doorway of Nos 108-19 Wentworth Model Dwellings in Goulston Street and noticed a piece of torn, bloodied apron on the floor that had not been there on his previous visit at 2.20 am. If the timing of Long's visits to the doorway are correct, the murderer would have spent forty minutes in the vicinity of his crime. Endacott would have had no need to move away from the area, as that was his beat.

Above the apron, on the black painted brick fascia of the doorway were written the words that over the years have been the cause of much contention.

> **The Juwes are**
> **The men that**
> **Will not**
> **be Blamed**
> **for nothing**

The inscription became the matter of immediate debate. Superintendent Thomas Arnold, head of H Division, was informed and, anxious to preserve the already fragile peace between the Jews and the rest of the public, sent an inspector to the scene armed with a sponge with orders to wait for his decision on whether the offending words should be erased. Superintendent Arnold arrived on the scene accompanied by Sir Charles Warren, who immediately agreed that the words should be removed, after a handwritten copy was made of them. The copy was taken down in the notebook of Constable Long and at the subsequent inquest into the death of Catherine Eddowes, Long admitted that he did not make a specific note of the spelling of the word JUWES. The Metropolitan Police and the Home Office agreed that the actual wording of the message was as above. The City Police on the other hand, said that the message read, 'The Juwes are not The men That Will be Blamed for nothing', thus putting a completely different interpretation to it. These differences have never been satisfactorily resolved as the words were erased by the Metropolitan Police at 5.30 am, despite the objections of the City Police, who thought that they should be photographed first.

Sir Charles Warren was criticised for having authorised the removal of what possibly could have been a clue left by the murderer, and was forced to send the following letter in which he explained his actions:

> I do not hesitate myself to say that if that writing had been left there would have been an onslaught upon the Jews, property would have been wrecked, and lives would probably have been lost; and I was much gratified with the promptitude with which Superintendent Arnold was prepared to act in the matter if I had not been there.

Regarding the piece of apron that was found under the message, Dr Brown later confirmed that it had been cut from Catherine's apron and used by the murderer to wipe the blood from his hands. His full report and his subsequent post-mortem is preserved at the Corporation of London Record Office. At this point I would like to thank the editors of *The Jack The Ripper A–Z* for their work in giving the correct punctuation to what were basically notes taken at the inquest. I would like to quote the almost whole of Dr Brown's inquest statement as I believe it gives credence to a theory I have that, despite Dr Brown's conclusions, Bowden Endacott did not work alone.

> The body was on its back, the head turned to the left shoulder. The arms by the side of the body as if they had fallen there. Both palms upwards, the fingers slightly bent.... Left leg extended in a line with the body. The abdomen was exposed. Right leg bent at the thigh and knee...

The throat cut across...

> The intestines were drawn out to a large extent and placed over the right shoulder – they were smeared over with some feculent matter. A piece of about two feet was quite detached from the body and placed between the body and the left arm, apparently by design. The lobe and auricle of the right ear was cut obliquely through.
>
> There was a quantity of clotted blood on the pavement on the left side of the neck round the shoulder and upper part of

the arm, and fluid blood-coloured serum which had flowed under the neck to the right shoulder, the pavement sloping in that direction.

Body was quite warm. No death stiffening had taken place. She must have been dead most likely within the half hour. We looked for superficial bruises and saw none. No blood on the skin of the abdomen or secretion of any kind on the thighs. No spurting of blood on the bricks or pavement around. No marks of blood below the middle of the body. Several buttons were found in the clotted blood after the body was removed. There was no blood on the front of the clothes. There were no traces of recent connection.

When the body arrived at Golden Lane [mortuary] ... . A piece of the deceased's ear dropped from the clothing.

I made a post-mortem examination at half past to on Sunday afternoon. Rigor mortis was well marked; body not quite cold. Green discoloration over the abdomen. ...

A bruise the size of a sixpence, recent and red, was discovered on the back of the left hand between the thumb and first finger. A few small bruises on the right shin of older date. The hands and arms were bronzed. No bruises on the scalp, the back of the body or the elbows.

The face was very much mutilated. There was a cut about a quarter of an inch through the lower left eyelid, dividing the structures completely through. The upper eyelid on that side, there was a scratch through the skin on the left upper eyelid, near to the angle of the nose. The right eyelid was cut through to about half an inch.

There was a deep cut over the bridge of the nose, extending from the left border of the nasal bone down near to the angle of the jaw on the right side of the cheek. This cut went into the bone and divided all the structures of the cheek except the mucous membrane of the mouth.

The tip of the nose was quite detached from the nose by an oblique cut from the bottom of the nasal bone to where the wings of the nose join on the face. A cut from this divided the upper lip and extended through the substance of the gum over the right upper lateral incisor tooth. About half an inch from the top of the nose was another oblique cut. There was a cut on the right angle of the mouth as if the cut of a point of a knife. The cut extended an inch and a half, parallel with lower lip.

There was on each side of the cheek a cut which peeled up the skin, forming a triangular flap about an inch and a half.

On the left cheek there were two abrasions of the epithelium ... under the left ear.

The throat was cut across to the extent of about six or seven inches. A superficial cut commenced about an inch and a half below the lobe below (and about two and a half inches behind) the left ear, and extended across the throat to about three inches below the lobe of right ear. The big muscle across the throat was divided through on the left side. The large vessels on the left side of the neck were severed. The larynx was severed below the vocal cord. All the deep structures were severed to the bone, the knife marking intervertebral cartilage's. The sheath of the vessels on the right side was just opened. The carotid artery had a fine hole opening. The internal jugular vein was opened an inch and a half – not divided. The blood vessels contained clot. All these injuries were performed by a sharp instrument like a knife, and pointed.

The cause of death was haemorrhage from the left common carotid artery. The death was immediate and the mutilations were inflicted after death.

We examined the abdomen. The front walls were laid open from the breast bone to the pubes. The cut commenced opposite the enciform cartilage. The incision went upwards, not penetrating the skin that was over the sternum. It then divided the enciform cartilage. The knife must have cut obliquely at the expense of the front surface of that cartilage.

Behind this, the liver was stabbed as if by the point of a sharp instrument. Below this was another incision into the liver of about two and a half inches, and below this the left lobe of the liver was slit through by a vertical cut. Two cuts were shewn by a jagging of the skin on the left side.

The abdominal walls were divided in the middle line to within a quarter of an inch of the navel. The cut then took a horizontal course for two inches and a half towards right side. It then divided round the navel on the left side, and made a parallel incision to the former horizontal incision, leaving the navel on a tongue of skin. Attached to the navel was two and a half inches of the lower part of the rectus muscle on the left side of the abdomen. The incision then took an oblique direction to the right and was shelving. The incision went down the right side of the vagina and rectum for half an inch behind the rectum.

There was a stab of about an inch on the left groin. This was done by a pointed instrument. Below this was a cut of three inches going through all tissues making a wound of the peritoneum [sc. perineum] about the same extent.

An inch below the crease of the thigh was a cut extending from the anterior spine if the ilium obliquely down the inner side of the left thigh and separating the left labium, forming a flap of skin up to the groin. The left rectus muscle was not detached.

There was a flap of skin formed from the right thigh, attaching the right labium, and extending up to the spine of the ilium. The muscles on the right side inserted into the frontal ligaments were cut through.

The skin was retracted through the whole of the cut in the abdomen, but the vessels were not clotted. Nor had there been any appreciable bleeding from the vessels. I drew the conclusion that the cut was made after death, and there would not be much blood on the murderer. The cut was made by some one on right side of the body, kneeling below the middle of the body...

The intestines had been detached to a large extent from the mesentery. About two feet of the colon was cut away. The sigmoid flexure was invaginated into the rectum very tightly.

Right kidney pale, bloodless, with slight congestion of the base of the pyramids.

There was a cut from the upper part of the slit on the under surface of the liver to the left side, and another cut at right angles to this, which were about an inch and a half deep and two and a half inches long. Liver itself was healthy.

The gall bladder contained bile. The pancreas was cut, but not through, on the left side of the spinal column. Three and a half inches of the lower border of the spleen by half an inch was attached only to the peritoneum.

The peritoneal lining was cut through on the left side and the left kidney carefully taken out and removed. The left renal artery was cut through. I should say that someone who knew the position of the kidney must have done it.

The lining membrane over the uterus was cut through. The womb was cut through horizontally, leaving a stump of three quarters of an inch. The rest of the womb had been taken away with some of the ligaments. The vagina and cervix of the womb was uninjured.

The bladder was healthy and uninjured, and contained three or four ounces of water. There was a tongue–like cut through the anterior wall of the abdominal aorta. The other organs were healthy.

There were no indications of connection.

I believe the wound on the throat was first inflicted. I believe she must have been lying on the ground.

The wounds on the face and the abdomen prove that they were inflicted by a sharp pointed knife, and that in the abdomen by one six inches long.

I believe the perpetrator of this act must have had considerable knowledge of the positions of the organs in the abdominal cavity and the way of removing them. The parts removed would be of no use for any professional purpose. It required a great deal of medical knowledge to have removed the kidney and to know where it was placed. Such knowledge might be possessed by some one in the habit of cutting up animals.

I think the perpetrator of this act had sufficient time, or he would not have nicked the lower eyelids. It would take at least five minutes.

I cannot assign any reason for the parts being taken away. I feel sure there was no struggle. I believe it was the act of one person.

The throat had been so instantly severed that no noise could have been emitted. I should not expect much blood to be found on the person who had inflicted these wounds…

My attention was called to the apron… . The blood spots were of recent origin. I have seen the portion of an apron produced by Dr Phillips and stated to have been found in Goulston Street. It is impossible to say it is human blood. I fitted the piece of apron which had a new piece of material on it which had evidently been sewn on to the piece I have, the seams of the borders of the two actually corresponding. Some blood and, apparently, faecal matter was found on the portion found in Goulston Street. I believe the wounds on the face to have been done to disfigure the corpse.

This document raises some interesting points. Dr Brown believed that the murderer must have had some medical knowledge in order for him to have found the left kidney, which is normally covered by a membrane, and then remove it. Other doctors disagreed saying they did not think the murderer indicated much expertise. The coroner, Wynne Baxter, described the murderer as an 'unskilled imitator' but Brown replied by saying that he must have had anatomical knowledge to be able to have identified the kidney and to have removed it. Bowden Endacott was brought up on a farm and his work with animals would have had given him the necessary knowledge to understand where the kidney was. At a later meeting held in 1905, Dr Brown stated that the Ripper had some knowledge of human anatomy, but used cuts suggestive of a butcher.

There is, however, another connection between Endacott and a doctor who was involved in the case of Catherine's missing left kidney. It is believed that a portion of the missing kidney was sent through the post to George Lusk, who was president of the Whitechapel Vigilance Committee. The 3in square cardboard box containing the grisly relic arrived at Mr Lusk's home on 16 October 1888. Accompanying it was a letter that read:

From hell

Mr Lusk
Sor
I send you half the Kidne I took from one woman prasarved it for you tother piece I fried and ate it was very nise I may send you the bloody knif that took it out if you only wate a whil longer.
Signed   Catch me when you can
                     Mishter Lusk.

The piece of kidney eventually found its way to Dr Thomas Horrocks Openshaw, who was curator of the Pathology Museum at London Hospital. Dr Openshaw stated that he thought the kidney was that of a 45-year-old woman who was afflicted with Bright's disease (inflammation of the kidneys). He also though it was a 'ginny' kidney (belonging to a heavy drinker) and had been removed from the body within the last three weeks. Although Openshaw later denied having said that it was a ginny kidney or that it showed signs of Bright's disease, Dr Brown's inquest report clearly shows that Catherine Eddowes was suffering from it, so it is more than likely that the kidney was in fact hers and the murderer wrote the letter.

The letter has been examined by the Canadian graphologist, C. M. MacLeod, who thought that the writer was aged 20–45 with rudimentary education, possibly a heavy drinker and cockily self-confident. He also thought the writing showed a mind with a vicious drive and great cunning, and was quite capable of conceiving and carrying out the murders. He also would have had enough brains to hold a steady job and be able to mask his true personality. All of this fits Bowden Endacott perfectly.

I am sure Endacott and Openshaw must have known each other. In 1881, Endacott, his wife Emily, and their son Bowden occupied 21 Gower Street in London. After Endacott's acquittal following the Cass case in 1887, he was put on special duty at the British Museum, just across the road from 21 Gower Street. Although he and his family were now living at 22 Colville Place, just off the Tottenham Court Road, he must have seen and spoken to the new occupant of his former home, Dr Thomas Horrocks Openshaw. All of this may be coincidental of course, but it all fits.

As far as Catherine Eddowes is concerned, the problem remains of exactly what she did in the last half hour of her life. There is no evidence that she ever prostituted herself. We know that she managed to find enough money to get drunk between the time she left John Kelly at 2.00 pm on the day before her death and 8.30 am on the day of her death, when she was arrested in Aldgate High Street. This could have come from prostitution, but she could also have borrowed it or even pawned something she owned. We also have Dr Brown's statement that no sexual intercourse had taken place immediately prior to her death so she evidently did not entertain a client. The only possible explanation is that she went to meet someone she knew, and she arranged to meet him at 1.30 am at the corner of Duke's Street and Church Passage, where they were seen, and that person murdered her. The only person she could have met and who had a good reason for being in the area was a police officer – Bowden Endacott.

Another point concerns part of the apron found in Goulston Street. A murderer would never intentionally leave a trail leading back to where he lived, that is obvious. The murderer had forty minutes to plan his escape route, but he was in no hurry as he had a perfectly good, legal reason for being in the area. The apron was found eastwards from where the murder was committed; Endacott lived north of the spot. It would have been logical of him to throw the apron down in a completely different direction from where he lived or, as in this case, from where he was working, at Bishopsgate Police Station. The writing on the wall could also have been a clever ploy to put his pursuers off the scent and give them something else to think about. Whatever actually happened we shall never truly know, but the only person that could have spent that much time in the vicinity of the crime and not have been suspected was a police officer.

Crowds lined the streets for the funeral procession of Catherine Eddowes when she was buried on 8 October 1888, in an unmarked grave at Little Ilford.

POSTSCRIPT

It is such a pity that so many records of the City Police relating to witness statements were lost during the Second World War. One in particular could have been of great relevance – that of James Blenkingsop, a nightwatchman who was on duty in St James's Place. He told the newspapers that at 1.30 am, a respectably dressed man approached him and asked, 'Have you seen a man and a woman go through here?' Blenkingsop said that he had seen some people pass but had not taken much notice. His story must have been investigated, but unfortunately the findings are no longer available so we are left with yet another mystery as to who the man was and why he asked such a significant question. The man could not have identified himself as being a police officer as Blenkingsop would have reported this fact to the newspaper. The only other possible explanation is the murderer did in fact have an accomplice, who was checking to see which way his partner had gone.

CHAPTER 10

Mary Jane Kelly – Murdered 9 November 1888

Mary Jane Kelly was the last official victim of Jack the Ripper. Her murder is also the most puzzling. Mary Kelly was the youngest of the victims, she was the only one to be murdered indoors, and the savagery of the attack left even the most seasoned officers who saw the body with nightmares for the rest of their lives.

It is obvious that Mary Jane Kelly knew the previous victims, and although it had been a month since the last murder, and life may have been getting back to normal in the East End, fear must have still been present.

The murderer must have been someone that Mary thought she could trust, or else why would she invite him back to her own room? This wasn't something a prostitute would have normally done. The most puzzling aspect of the murder is this: was it actually Mary Jane Kelly that was murdered?

The story that Kelly gave her friends was that she had been born in Limerick, Ireland, in 1863. As a child, her father moved the family to Wales where he took a job in an ironworks. In 1879, she said that she married a man named Davies, who died in a pit accident two or three years later. She then moved to a cousin's house in Cardiff where she became a prostitute, although the Cardiff police had no record of her having been there. Mary also said that she was ill and spent nearly a year in an infirmary in Cardiff, although none of this can be confirmed as most of it was told by Kelly to the man she lived with just before her murder, Joseph Barnett.

She went on to say that she came to London in 1884, and worked in a high-class brothel in the West End. During this time, she said that she drove around in a carriage and went to Paris with a gentleman, but returned after a short while, as she did not like France. How she ended up in the East End is not known, but after returning from France it is believed she went to stay in lodgings at St George's Street, in the Ratcliff Highway district.

A reporter who had been looking into the murder of Mary Jane Kelly, wrote:

> It would appear that on her arrival in London she made the acquaintance of a French woman residing in the neighbourhood of Knightsbridge, who, she informed her friends, led her to pursue the degraded life which had now culminated in her untimely end. She made no secret of the fact that while she was with this woman she would drive about in a carriage and made several journeys to the French capital, and, in fact, led a life which is described as that 'of a lady'. By some means, however, at present, not exactly clear, she suddenly drifted into the East End. Here fortune failed her and a career that stands out in bold and sad contrast to her earlier experience was commenced. Her experiences with the East End appears to have begun with a woman [according to press reports a Mrs Buki] who resided in one of the thoroughfares off Ratcliff (e) Highway, known as St. George's Street. This person appears to have received Kelly direct from the West End home, for she had not been there very long when, it is stated, both women went to the French lady's residence and demanded the box which contained numerous dresses of a costly description.

Mary Jane started to drink and this made her unwelcome at Mrs Buki's, so she went to stay at a Mrs Carthy's at Breezer's Hill, off Pennington Street. Mrs Carthy said that she believed Mary, or Marie Jeanette, as she liked to call herself, came from 'well-to-do people'. This information probably only came from a story that Mary told her, but there was doubt as to Mary's origins. Some press reports suggested that Kelly was not her real surname, and that she had taken it from a common-law husband. It was said that Joseph Barnett used the name as an alias from time to time. Mrs Carthy also stated that Mary was 'an excellent scholar and an artist of no mean degree'. However, as Joseph Barnett describes Mrs Carthy's house as a 'bad house', it is not safe to assume that what Mrs Carthy was referring to – and taking into account the Victorian penchant for all sorts of sexual deviancy – she could have meant that Mary had been a quick learner in the ways of a prostitute and very good at her job.

Sometime between 1885 and 1886, Mary lived with a man named Morganstone near Stepney Gasworks, and then met and had a relationship with a man named Joseph Fleming who, according to Mrs Carthy, wanted to marry her. It is believed that Mary remained very fond of Joseph Fleming even after they split up, and the friendship continued after she moved in with Joseph Barnett. She met Barnett on 8 April 1887, when she was living at

Mary Jane Kelly – Murdered 9 November 1888

Cooly's Common Lodging House in Thrawl Street, Spitalfields. Their first home was in George Street, which lay between Thrawl Street and Flower and Dean Street, then they moved to Little Paternoster Row, Dorset Street, until they were evicted for drunken behaviour and not paying the rent. By February or March of 1888, they had moved to 13 Miller's Court, Dorset Street, which was the back room of 26 Dorset Street. The rent was 4/6d (22½p) a week and by the time Mary was murdered they were 28/- (£1.40) in arrears.

Miller's Court was on the opposite side of the road to Crossinghams Lodging House, where Annie Chapman had lived. The court was reached by means of a 3ft-wide opening between numbers 26 and 27 Dorset Street (which no longer exists but can be seen at the back of the car park that fronts on to White's Row) and it was the first opening on the right coming from Commercial Street. There were six houses in the court, each of them let by John McCarthy who owned a chandler's shop at 27 Dorset Street. Mary Kelly's house was partitioned off from the rest of the building and was entered from a door at the end of the arched passage. As it was the first door on the right in the court, anyone entering or leaving the court would have to pass it.

The room they lived in was about 12ft square. Directly opposite the door was a fireplace and on the left of the door and at right angles to it were two windows, from one of which it was possible to reach through and unbolt the door. To the right of the door stood a small bedside table that was hit each time the door was opened. Next to the table was a bed with its head against the door wall and its side against the right wall. The room also contained two other small tables and a chair and by the fireplace was a small cupboard that contained some crockery, empty ginger beer bottles, and some stale bread. The window closest to the door was broken. Mary had damaged it whilst drunk several weeks before the murder, and in place of the pane of glass hung a man's overcoat.

In his statement made to the police, Joseph Barnett said that he had lost his job at Billingsgate Market and, after an argument with Mary on 30 October 1888 about her prostituting herself again and letting prostitutes stay in the room with her, they separated. Barnett went to live at Mrs Buller's boarding house at 24-25 New Street, Bishopsgate, but continued to visit Mary on an almost daily basis to give her what money and help he could. He later said to the newspapers:

> She would never have gone wrong again, and I shouldn't have left her if it had not been for the prostitutes stopping at the

> house. She only let them stay because she was good hearted and did not like to refuse them shelter on cold bitter nights. We lived comfortably until Marie [his name for her] allowed a prostitute named Julia to sleep in the same room; I objected; and as Mrs Harvey afterwards came and stayed there, I left and took lodgings elsewhere.

The 'Julia', he was referring to is believed to have been Julia Van Turney, who lived at 1 Miller's Court, although this is not certain. Mrs Harvey is believed to have been Maria Harvey who lived at 3 New Court, Dorset Street. Harvey said that she slept with Mary on the nights of Monday 5 and Tuesday 6 November. The exact connection between the two women is not known, but it has been suggested that a possible lesbian relationship took place.

Some confusion then arose because Harvey said she was with Mary on the afternoon and evening of Thursday 8 November, when Joseph Barnett called. Another friend of Mary's, Lizzie Albrook, said that it was she who was there. Speaking of Mary, Lizzie Albrook later said:

> About the last thing she said to me was, 'Whatever you do don't you do wrong and turn out as I have.' She had often spoken to me in this way and warned me against going on the streets as she had done. She told me; too, that she was heartily sick of the life she was leading and wished she had money enough to go back to Ireland where her people lived [thus inferring that either Mary's family had returned to Ireland from Wales, or, that Mary had lied about her family going to Wales in the first place]. I do not believe she would have gone out as she did if she had not been obliged to do so to keep herself from starvation.

Harvey later told the press that she had spent the afternoon with Mary who had come to visit her in New Court and they then went drinking and separated at about 7.30 pm. Harvey said that Mary went in the direction of Leman Street, which she was in the habit of frequenting (soliciting). However, Joseph Barnett said that he called on Mary between 7.30 pm and 7.45 pm and stated that it was Maria Harvey he saw there. Although these contradictory accounts are not of great importance to us in the chronology of the last few hours of Mary's life, it does show the difficulty the police must have had in trying to piece together her whereabouts. For example, another friend of Mary's, Elizabeth Foster, said she was drinking with her in The Ten Bells on Thursday evening but made no mention of Maria Harvey. Mary was also reportedly seen in The Britannia at 1.00 pm, in the company of a young man with a moustache. Yet another acquaintance of Mary's stated that he saw her in The Horn of Plenty with a man named Danny, who was said to be Joseph Barnett's brother, and 'Julia' (Van Turney?)

Whatever she was doing on the night of her death, the next sighting of her was at 11.45 pm, when Mary Ann Cox saw her return to Miller's Court. Mary Ann Cox lived at 5 Miller's Court and described herself as 'a widow and an unfortunate' (prostitute). She said that Mary had been wearing a linsey frock and a red knitted crossover shawl. She had spoken to Mary, who was drunk, and Mary had told her that she was going to sing: between midnight and 1.00 am several people heard her singing the song *A Violet from Mother's Grave.*

The next sighting of Mary Kelly was at 2.00 am. George Hutchinson, a labourer living at Victoria Home in Commercial Street, made the following statement to the police on 12 November:

> About 2 a.m. 9th I was coming by Thrawl Street, Commercial Street, and just before I got to Flower and Dean Street, I met the murdered woman Kelly, and she said to me, 'Hutchinson will you lend me sixpence?' I said 'I can't I have spent all my money going down to Romford'; she said 'good morning I must go and find some money.' She went away toward Thrawl Street. A man coming in the opposite direction to Kelly, tapped her on the shoulder and said something to her, they both burst out laughing. I heard her say 'alright' to him, and the man said 'you will be alright, for what I have told you': he then placed his right hand around her shoulders. He also had a kind of small parcel in his left hand, with a kind of strap round it. I stood against the lamp of the Queen's Head Public House, and watched him. They both then came past me and the man hung down his head, with, his hat over his eyes. I stooped down and looked him in the face. He looked at me stern. They both went into Dorset Street. I followed them. They both stood at the corner of the court for about three minutes. He said something to her. She said, 'alright my dear come along you will be comfortable.' He then placed his arm on her shoulder and she gave him a kiss. She said she had lost her handkerchief. He then pulled his handkerchief, a red one, and gave it to her. They both then went up the court together. I then went to the court to see if I could see them but I could not. I stood there for about three quarters of an hour to see if they came out. They did not so I went away.

Hutchinson later gave a description of the man, saying that he was of Jewish appearance, wearing a long dark coat with astrakhan collar and cuffs, dark jacket and trousers, light waistcoat, a dark felt hat, button boots and gaiters with white buttons. He had a linen collar and was wearing a black tie with a horseshoe pin through it. Hutchinson said that he was about 34 or 35, 5ft 6ins, pale complexion, dark hair and eyelashes and a slight moustache that was curled up at the ends.

During the next few hours, a number of witnesses saw various men in and around Miller's Court. Shortly before 4.00 am, three women who lived in the court all reported hearing a cry of 'Murder!' coming from the direction of Mary's room but, as one of the witnesses noted, 'It is nothing unusual in the street. I did not take particular notice.'

At 10.45 am the following day, Thomas Bowyer was sent to Mary's to collect the outstanding rent, by the landlord John McCarthy. After knocking on the door and getting no answer he pulled back the coat covering the broken window. What he saw horrified him:

> I saw two pieces of flesh lying on the table... . The second time I looked I saw a body on this bed, and blood on the floor. I at once went very quietly to Mr McCarthy. We then stood in the shop and I told him what I had seen. We both went to the police-station, but first of all we both went to the window, and McCarthy looked in to satisfy himself. We told the inspector at the police-station of what we had seen. Nobody else knew of the matter. The inspector returned with us.

John McCarthy made the following statement at the inquest:

> I looked through the window and saw a lot of blood and everything. I said to my man 'Don't tell any one let us fetch the police.' I knew deceased as Mary Jane Kelly. I have seen the body and have no doubt as to the identity. I and Bowyer went then to the Police Court Commercial Street and saw Inspector Beck ... I told Inspector Beck what I had seen. He put on his hat and coat and came with me at once. Deceased has lived in the room with Joe for ten months both together. They lived comfortably together but once broke the two windows. The furniture and everything in the room belongs to me. I was paid 4/6d a week for the room but rent was 28/– in arrear. The rent was paid to me weekly, the room was let weekly.
>
> I very often saw deceased worse for drink. She was a very quiet woman when sober but noisy when in drink. She was not ever helpless when drunk.

As we shall see later, Dr Thomas Bond, the A Division police surgeon who examined the body, said he thought Mary had been murdered in the early hours of the morning. The inquest however,

Mary Jane Kelly – Murdered 9 November 1888

was totally disrupted when an acquaintance of Mary's, Caroline Maxwell, made the following statement:

> I live at 14 Dorset Street. My husband's name is Harry Maxwell. He is a Lodging House Deputy. I knew deceased for about four months as Mary Jane. I also knew Joe Barnett. I believe she was an unfortunate girl. I never spoke to her except twice.
>
> I took a deal of notice of deceased this evening [*sic*] seeing her standing at the corner of the Court on Friday from 8 to half past. I know the time by taking the plates my husband had to take care of from the house opposite. I am positive the time was between 8 & half past. I am positive I saw deceased. I spoke to her. I said, 'Why Mary. What brings you up so early?' She said, 'Oh! I do feel so bad. Oh Carry [*sic*] I feel so bad!' She knew my name. I asked her to have a drink, she said, 'Oh no I have just had a drink of ale and have brought it all up.' It was in the road. I saw it. As she said this she motioned with her head and I concluded she meant she had been to the Britannia at the corner. I left her saying I pitied her feelings. I then went to Bishopsgate as I returned I saw her outside the Britannia talking to a man. The time was then about 20 minutes to half an hour later, about a quarter to nine. I could not describe the man. I did not pass them. I went into my house. I saw them in the distance, I am certain it was deceased. The man was not a tall man. He had on dark clothes and a sort of plaid coat. I could not say what hat he had on. Mary Jane had a dark skirt, velvet body, and marone [maroon] shawl and no hat.
>
> I have seen deceased in drink but not really drunk.

As this was a crucial piece of information, the coroner questioned the validity of her statement saying, 'You must be very careful about your evidence, because it is different to other people's.' She reiterated what she saw adding that she couldn't describe the man as 'they were at some distance', adding 'I am sure it was the deceased. I am willing to swear it.'

Her testimony has resulted in a countless number of theories being put forward. One of these is that Caroline Maxwell was mistaken in her identification, or about the date she spoke to Mary. However, Inspector Abberline went back to see her following the inquest and tried again and again to get her to say that she had possibly been mistaken about the date. Mrs Maxwell stuck to her story and Abberline went back to Scotland Yard and said to colleagues that he thought the woman was telling the truth but that there must be some logical explanation.

One of the logical explanations put forward was that the murderer was a woman, who dressed up in Mary's clothes to make her escape. Although why she would have hung around after the murder was not explained. It has also been suggested that the body found was not that of Mary Jane Kelly, but a friend of hers. If so, once again we come back to the fact that if Mary knew that her friend was lying dead in her room, she must have had a very cool presence of mind to stand around talking to Caroline Maxwell.

If we assume that Maxwell was correct in her statement, Dr Bond must have been wrong in his assumption about the time of death, and Thomas Bowyer must have found the body shortly after she was murdered. If, however, Maxwell was wrong about the date, then questions that were put to Mary Ann Cox at the inquest play a great part in my theory about the identity of Jack the Ripper.

> Coroner: 'How many men live in the court who work in Spitalfields Market?'
> Cox: 'One. At a quarter-past six I heard a man go down the court. That was too late for the market.'
> Coroner: 'From what house did he go?'
> Cox: 'I don't know.'
> Coroner: 'Did you hear the door bang after him?'
> Cox: 'No.'
> Coroner: 'Then he must have walked up the court and back again?'
> Cox: 'Yes.'
> Coroner: 'It might have been a policeman?'
> Cox: 'It might have been.'

The coroner was undoubtedly trying to ascertain the truth in what must have been a difficult inquest with all the contradictory statements that had been put forward. But why would he think it must have been a policeman who walked down the court at that time? Did the police have their own suspicions about the murderer being one of their own? Were they trying to prove he had been there so they would have some evidence and then they could question him?

After the police arrived at Miller's Court to look at the body, a substantial delay occurred when they were informed that two bloodhounds, Burgho and Barnaby, were being sent to try and pick up the trail of the murderer. It was not until 1.30 pm that Superintendent Arnold arrived from H Division and said that the dogs would not be coming. He ordered John McCarthy to break open the door, which McCarthy did with the aid of an axe handle. The true horror of what they saw is summed up best in Walter Dew's memoir when he said the sight of Kelly's body was imprinted on his mind for the rest of his life, that he could not venture into the East End without recalling the memory, and thus he avoided the area whenever he could.

Dr Thomas Bond gave the following report to the inquest:

> The body was lying naked in the middle of the bed, the shoulders flat, but the axis of the body inclined to the left side of the bed. The head was turned on the left cheek. The left arm was close to the body with the forearm flexed at a right angle & lying across the abdomen. The right arm was slightly abducted from the body & rested on the mattress, the elbow bent & the forearm supine with the fingers clenched. The legs were wide apart, the left thigh at right angles to the trunk & the right forming an obtuse angle with the pubes.
>
> The whole of the surface of the abdomen & thighs was removed & the abdominal Cavity emptied of its viscera. The breast were cut off, the arms mutilated by several jagged wounds & the face hacked beyond recognition of the features. The tissues of the neck were severed all round down to the bone.
>
> The viscera were found in various parts viz: the uterus & Kidneys with one breast under the head, the other breast by the Rt foot, the Liver between the feet, the intestines by the right side & the spleen by the left side of the body. The flaps removed from the abdomen and thighs were on a table.
>
> The bed clothing at the right corner was saturated with blood, & on the floor beneath was a pool of blood covering about 2 feet square. The wall by the right side of the bed & in line with the neck was marked by blood which had struck in a number of separate splashes.
>
> Post-mortem examination
>
> The face was gashed in all directions, the nose, cheeks, eyebrows and ears being partly removed. The lips were blanched & cut by several incisions running obliquely down to the chin. There were also numerous cuts extending irregularly across all the features.
>
> The neck was cut through the skin & other tissues right down to the vertebrae the 5th & 6th being deeply notched. The skin cuts in the front of the neck showed distinct ecchymosis.
>
> The air passage was cut at the lower part of the larynx through the cricoid cartilage.
>
> Both breasts were removed by more by more or less circular incisions, the muscles down to the ribs being attached to the breasts. The intercostals between the 4th, 5th and 6th ribs were cut through & the contents of the thorax visible through the openings.

The skin & tissues of the abdomen from the costal arch to the pubes were removed in three large flaps. The right thigh was denuded in front to the bone, the flap of skin, including the external organs of generation & part of the right buttock. The left thigh was stripped of skin, fascia & muscles as far as the knee.

The left calf showed a long gash through skin & tissues to the deep muscles & reaching from the knee to 5 ins above the ankle.

Both arms & forearms had extensive & jagged wounds.

The right thumb showed a small superficial incision about 1 in long, with extravasation of blood in the skin & there were several abrasions on the back of the hand moreover showing the same condition.

On opening the thorax it was found that the right lung was minimally adherent by old firm adhesions. The lower part of the lung was broken & torn away.

The left lung was intact: it was adherent at the apex & there were a few adhesions over the side. In the substances of the lung were several nodules of consolidation.

The Pericardium was open below & the Heart absent.

In the abdominal cavity was some partly digested food of fish & potatoes & similar food was found in the remains of the stomach attached to the intestines.

Dr Bond made the error of describing the body as naked, when in fact the photograph taken at the scene shows that she was wearing the remains of a chemise or underslip.

In a report he made to Sir Robert Anderson, Dr Bond gives his estimation as to the time of death, and his own overview of the previous murders. Anderson specifically asked for the report so we must assume that he valued Bond's opinion. An assumption verified by Anderson asking for Bond's opinions on two further murders, which we shall examine later. On the general pattern of the previous murders however, Bond's views contradicted those of Dr Phillips, who said he thought the murders were not all by the same hand. Whilst Bond's report sheds no light on the actual murderer, his psychological profile of the killer is interesting:

1. All [canonical] five murders were no doubt committed by the same hand. In the first four the throats appear to have been cut from left to right. In the last case owing to the extensive mutilation it is impossible to say in what direction the fatal cut was made, but arterial blood was found on the wall in splashes close to where the woman's head must have been lying.

2. All the circumstances surrounding the murders lead me to form the opinion that the woman must have been lying down when murdered and in every case the throat was first cut.

3. In the four murders of which I have seen the notes only, I cannot form a very definite opinion as to the time that had elapsed between the murder and the discovering of the body. In one case, that of Berner's [*sic*] Street, the discovery appears to have been made immediately after the deed – in Buck's Row, Hanbury Street, and Mitre Square three or four hours only could have elapsed. In the Dorset Street Case the body was lying on the bed at the time of my visit, two o'clock, quite naked and mutilated as in the annexed report –

Rigor Mortis had set in, but increased during the progress of the examination. From this it is difficult to say with any degree of certainty the exact time that had elapsed since death as the period varies from 6 to 12 hours before rigidity sets in. The body was comparatively cold at 2 o'clock and the remains of a recently taken meal were found in the stomach and scattered about over the intestines. It is, therefore, pretty certain that the woman must have been dead about twelve hours and the partly digested food would indicate that death took place about 3 or 4 hours after food was taken, so 1 or 2 o'clock in the morning would be the probable time of the murder.

4. In all the cases there appears to be no evidence of struggling and the attacks were probably so sudden and made in such a position that the women could neither resist nor cry out. In the Dorset Street case the corner of the sheet to the right of the woman's head was much cut and saturated with blood, indicating that the face may have been covered with the sheet at the time of the attack.

5. In the first four cases the murderer must have attacked from the right side of the victim. In the Dorset Street case, he must have attacked in front or from the left, as there would be no room for him between the wall and the part of the bed on which the woman was lying. Again, the blood had flowed down on the right side of the woman and spurted on to the wall.

6. The murderer would not necessarily be splashed or deluged with blood, but his hands and arms must have been covered and parts of his clothing must certainly have been smeared with blood.

7. The mutilations in each case excepting the Berner's [*sic*] Street one were all of the same character and showed clearly that in all the murders the object was mutilation.

8. In each case the mutilation was inflicted by a person who had no scientific nor anatomical knowledge. In my opinion he does not even possess the technical knowledge of a butcher or horse slaughterer or any person accustomed to cut up dead animals.
9. The instrument must have been a strong knife at least six inches long, very sharp, pointed at the top and about an inch in width. It may have been a clasp knife, a butcher's knife or a surgeon's knife. I think it was no doubt a straight knife.
10. The murderer must have been a man of physical strength and of great coolness and daring. There is no evidence that he had an accomplice. He must in my opinion be a man subject to periodical attacks of Homicidal and erotic mania. The character of the mutilations indicate that the man may be in a condition sexually, that may be called satyriasis. It is of course possible that the Homicidal impulse may have developed from a revengeful or brooding condition of the mind, or that Religious Mania may have been the original disease, but I do not think either hypothesis is likely. The murderer in external appearance is quite likely to be a quiet inoffensive looking man probably middle-aged and neatly and respectably dressed. I think he must be in the habit of wearing a cloak or overcoat or he could hardly have escaped notice in the street if the blood on his hands or clothes were visible.
11. Assuming the murderer to be such a person as I have just described he would probably be solitary and eccentric in his habits, also he is most likely to be a man without regular occupation, but with some small income or pension. He is possibly living among respectable persons who have some knowledge of his character and habits and may have grounds for suspicion that he is not quite right in his mind at times. Such persons would probably be unwilling to communicate suspicions to the Police for fear of trouble or notoriety, whereas if there were a prospect of reward it might overcome their scruples.

It is worth noting that Dr Bond's profile of the murderer almost matches entirely the one the FBI compiled in 1988 and, more importantly, fits what I know to be the psychological behaviour of Bowden Endacott.

Dr Bond's theory about the time of death raises some interesting points. When the room was first entered it was found that a fire had been lit in the fireplace and some clothing had been destroyed, although Mary Kelly's clothes were on a chair at the foot of the bed. Maria Harvey later claimed that she had left two men's shirts, a boy's shirt, a black crepe bonnet, a child's petticoat, a man's overcoat and a pawn ticket in Mary's room. Only the overcoat was ever returned to her and the police believed that the murderer had burned the clothes to illuminate the room. The point of this is that the tremendous heat created in a room only about 12ft by 10ft – so much that the police believed it was sufficient to have burned the spout and handle of a kettle that was found near the fire – would have altered the process of rigor mortis. Although Dr Bond was undoubtedly an excellent doctor and surgeon, he was not fortunate enough to have the knowledge of today's forensic scientist.

We now know that in very hot conditions rigor mortis can occur very quickly. Dr Bond also took his observations as to the time of death from the remains of a meal found in the stomach. However, it is now accepted that the rate of digestion varies from person to person so this is not a good guideline.

Modern forensic testing has shown that in a body in which rigor mortis has set in, and the body is still comparatively warm, death must have occurred three to eight hours previously.

Taking the fact that rigor mortis had set in when Dr Bond began his examination at 2.00 pm and, as he said it was 'comparatively cold' (i.e. still warm), and taking into account the heat in the room, the murder must have taken place between 6.00 pm and 10.30 am when the body was found. This would fit in with the statements of Mary Ann Cox and the policeman in the court, and that of Caroline Maxwell, who reported seeing Mary between 8.00 am and 9.00 am.

Although this does not get us any nearer to identifying the murderer it does help in cutting down the timespan in which the murder was committed.

Mary Ann Kelly was buried on 19 November 1888, in Leytonstone Roman Catholic Cemetery. Despite widespread press coverage, no members of her family attended the funeral. Her preferred name, 'Marie Jeanette', was engraved on her coffin and entered on her death certificate. She would have liked that.

CHAPTER 11

The Other Victims

It is known that a serial killer often builds up to his first killing by attacking a victim without resorting to murder, and a number of attacks took place in an around the Whitechapel area of London preceding and following the aforementioned murders.

By the time of the latter cases, however, the police were reasonably convinced that because the timespan separating the murders was so great, they could not be attributed to the Ripper. Yet, what we now know from psychological studies of serial killers is that after the compulsion to kill overtakes him, the killer usually experiences a feeling of relief, and a 'cooling off' period ensues. Then, as the compulsion gradually overtakes him (for it is almost always a him) again, his anger and frustration come to the fore, until eventually it is time to go in search of another victim.

Although the earlier attacks on women are not usually associated with the work of the Ripper, they are worth looking into. Indeed, two attacks that took place shortly before the murder of Martha Tabram have led to speculation that they could have been the Ripper, doing, for want of a synonym, a 'trial run'.

Annie Millwood was the 38-year-old widow of a soldier named Richard Millwood. She lived at 8 White's Row, which runs parallel with Dorset Street in Spitalfields, where the murder of Mary Jane Kelly occurred and it is possible that she could also have been a prostitute. On Saturday, 25 February 1888, she was admitted to the Whitechapel Workhouse infirmary with what were described as 'stabs' to the lower legs and torso. Annie made a complete recovery from the attack, was released from the infirmary on 21 March, and was sent to the South Grove Workhouse in the Mile End Road. Ten days later she died in the back yard of the infirmary whilst 'engaged in some occupation'. Coroner Wynne Baxter attributed her death to 'sudden effusion into the pericardium from the rupture of the left pulmonary artery through ulceration.' The death was put down to natural causes, unrelated to her attack.

The Evening Post published the following report:

> It appears the deceased was admitted to the Whitechapel Infirmary suffering from numerous stabs in the legs and lower part of the body. She stated that she had been attacked by a

man who she did not know, and who stabbed her with a clasp knife which he took from his pocket. No one appears to have seen the attack, and as far as at present ascertained there is only the woman's statement to bear out the allegations of an attack, though that she had been stabbed cannot be denied.

There are similarities between this attack and that of Martha Tabram. She was aged 38, Martha was 39; White's Row was only minutes away from George Yard; the use of a clasp knife – some of Martha's injuries could have been made with the same type of knife.

The second attack was on Ada Wilson, a seamstress, living at 19 Maidman Street, Mile End. It was reported that Ada answered a knock on her door to find a man aged about 30 standing there, he was about 5ft 6ins, with a sunburned face and a fair moustache. The man forced his way into the room and demanded money. When she refused, he stabbed her twice in the throat and ran away, thinking she was dead. Luckily Ada survived the attack. Her description of the attacker fitted later descriptions of several of the men seen with Ripper victims, although the police made no link between her attack and those of the Ripper. It should be noted as a form of self-description, prostitutes often used the term 'seamstress'.

Theorists have said that she could not have been attacked by the Ripper, as robbery seemed to be the main motive. However, Bowden Endacott was never promoted in his career and, as a lowly security guard, would have almost definitely been in need of money. Additionally, in his disturbed state of mind, the connection between the woman whom he believed was a prostitute – and who had therefore caused his financial difficulties – could have been part of the motive for the attack on Ada Wilson.

Two later victims, Rose Mylett and Alice McKenzie, were also possibly attacked by the Ripper. Robert Anderson specifically asked Dr Bond to make a report on the deaths of these two women. In the case of Rose Mylett, Dr Bond disagreed with the findings of the K Division Metropolitan Police surgeon, Dr Matthew Brownfield, who thought that Rose had been strangled. Bond believed her death had been accidental.

Rose Mylett was a known prostitute who was born in Spitalfields in 1862. Not a lot is known about her early life apart from the few details given by her mother who said that Rose had been married to an upholsterer named Davis and had given birth to a son, who was seven at the time of her death. Rose lived off and on at her mother's in Pelham Street off Brick Lane, Spitalfields, at 18 George Street, off Flower and Dean Street, and in the Limehouse district.

At 7.55 pm on 19 December 1888, Rose was seen talking to two sailors in Poplar High Street, near Clarke's Yard, by Charles Ptolomey, an infirmary night attendant. He thought that Rose was sober and he heard her saying 'No, no, no!' to one of the sailors. The sailor's manner was suspicious enough for Ptolomey to remember the incident. At 2.30 am, Rose was seen by a woman named Alice Graves outside The George Public House in Commercial Road. She was drunk.

At 4.15 am, PC Robert Goulding found Rose's body in Clarke's Yard, which was situated between 184 and 186 Poplar High Street. Goulding said that the body, which was lying on its left side with the left leg drawn up and the right leg stretched out, was reminiscent of that of a Ripper victim although there were no obvious signs of injury and the clothes were not disarranged. However, he later said his initial thought was that she had died of natural causes. This could have been in response to orders from his superiors, due to the later disagreement as to Rose's actual cause of death. Although the body was found two miles from the centre of the Whitechapel murders, as the Ripper had waited a month between the murders of Elizabeth Stride and Catherine Eddowes, and then Mary Jane Kelly, it soon got people asking the question, had the Ripper struck again?

Mr Harris, Dr Brownfield's assistant, confirmed that she was dead, but no one could work out how she had died, until a small mark that could have been the imprint of a piece of string was found on her neck.

Dr Brownfield conducted the post-mortem and his report reads as follows:

> Blood was oozing from the nostrils, and there was a slight abrasion on the right side of the face.... . On the neck there was a mark which had evidently been caused by cord drawn tightly round the neck, from the spine to the left ear. Such a mark would be made by a four-thread cord. There were also impressions of the thumbs and middle and index fingers of some person plainly visible on each side of the neck. There were no injuries to the arms or legs. The brain was gorged with an almost black fluid blood. The stomach was full of meat and potatoes, which had only recently been eaten. Death was due to strangulation. Deceased could not have done it herself. The marks on her neck were probably caused by her trying to pull the cord off. ... the murderer must have stood at the left rear of the woman, and, having the ends of the cord round his hands, thrown it round her throat, crossed his hands, and thus strangled her. If it had been done in this way, it would account for the mark not going completely round her neck.

The police however, were not convinced that it was murder. Anderson had been to Clarke's Yard and had found no signs of a struggle, no cord, her clothing had not been torn and he found no second set of footprints anywhere in the soft ground where that body had lain. He also though that the body 'lay naturally' on the ground. Anderson asked Dr Bond to examine the body and make a report. Instead, Dr Bond's assistant, Mr Harris and the police surgeon Alexander McKeller went to examine the body. They both thought that death was due to strangulation. Eventually Anderson insisted that Dr Bond examine the body personally, which he did. His first report tentatively supported the post-mortem report of Dr Brownfield. Anderson asked him to examine the body again and this time he came to the conclusion that Rose had choked to death whilst drunk, and the mark on her neck had been caused by her stiff velvet collar. He believed this because he said that when he looked for the ligature marks on her neck, they had disappeared and he had not noticed any additional signs of strangulation, such as a protruding tongue or clenched fists.

The medical reports also conflicted with two aspects of the witness statements. The first was that no alcohol was found in Rose's stomach, which contradicted Alice Grave's testimony that she said she had seen Rose drunk outside The George. The second was that Rose had never given birth, which conflicted Rose's mother's testimony that Rose had given birth to a son in 1881.

At the inquest, Wynne Baxter protested at the interference by the medical profession and wanted nothing to do with this 'nonsense' of 'death by natural causes'. In his summing up, he said:

> After Dr Brownfield and his assistant, duly qualified men, came to the conclusion that this was a case of homicidal strangulation, someone had a suspicion that the evidence was not satisfactory. At all events, you've heard that doctor after doctor went down to view the body without my knowledge or sanction as coroner. I did not wish to make that a personal matter, but I have never received such treatment before. Of the five doctors who saw the body, Dr Bond was the only one who considered the case was not one of murder. Dr Bond did not see the body until five days after her death and he was, therefore, at a disadvantage. Dr Bond stated that if this was a case of strangulation he should have expected to find the skin broken, but it was clearly shown, on reference being made to the records of the Indian doctors in the cases of Thug murders, that there were no marks whatever left. Other eminent authorities agreed with that view.

Dr Phillips, who was at the inquest, agreed with Baxter's summing up and noted that he thought that there had been signs of strangulation on the body of Annie Chapman.

The jury sided with Baxter and reached the verdict that Rose Mylett had died of 'wilful murder by person or persons unknown'. The police refused to accept the findings of the jury and did not pursue their investigations into the identity of the murderer. In his memoir, Anderson wrote, 'the Poplar case of December 1888, was death from natural causes, and but for the "Jack the Ripper" scare, no one would have thought of suggesting that it was homicide.'

Whatever Anderson's views, Rose Mylett's name was still included on a list of 'alleged' victims of the Ripper, held at Scotland Yard.

The murder of Alice McKenzie on Wednesday, 17 July 1889, again raised differences of opinions between the police and doctors. Alice, also known as 'Clay Pipe Alice', due to her preference for smoking a clay pipe, was believed to have been born in Peterborough in 1849. She moved to the East End some time before 1874, and in 1883 she began living with a porter named John McCormack, who worked for Jewish tailors in Hanbury Street. From around April 1889, the couple were living with a Mr Tenpenny's lodging house in Gun Street, off Artillery Lane, in Spitalfields.

Incidentally, Gun Street is still in existence in exactly the same appearance as it was then and the area encompassing Artillery Lane and Gun Street is often used by television and film companies when they are looking for locations that give a fairly accurate idea of what the streets in Victorian London were like. The area is well worth a visit.

A woman named Elizabeth Ryder managed the lodging house in Gun Street, and whilst she was there Alice worked as a charwoman and washerwoman, primarily for the Jewish residents of the area. The police, however, considered her a habitual prostitute.

At 4.00 pm on Tuesday, 16 July 1889, McCormack came home from work somewhat drunk and went to bed. Before he did so he gave Alice one shilling to spend on herself and 8d to pay Mrs Ryder the rent. McCormack said this was the last time he saw Alice alive, but Mrs Ryder stated that she saw Alice leave the house at Gun Street at about 8.30 pm and had heard McCormack and Alice arguing, so it seems that possibly McCormack was trying to make sure he would not be incriminated in Alice's murder by saying he had not spoken to her since 4.00 pm. A rumour was reported in *The Pall Mall Gazette* that sometime during the following few hours Alice was seen in the Royal Cambridge Music Hall with a blind boy named George Discon, or Dixon, who also lived at the lodging house. The newspaper said that after taking him home to the lodging house, Alice went out again to meet a man she had met in the music hall.

Between 11.30 pm and midnight Alice was seen 'walking hurriedly' along Flower and Dean Street by three friends of hers, Margaret Franklin, Sarah Marney, or Mahoney, and Catherine Hughes. Margaret asked her how she was and Alice said, 'All right. I can't stop now.' The women all stated that Alice seemed in a hurry.

At 12.15 am on 17 July, PC Joseph Allen, 423H, stopped to eat a snack under a street lamp in Castle Alley, which runs in a northerly direction off Whitechapel High Street. He said that the alley was deserted, but after about five minutes he saw another policeman enter the alley. This officer was PC Walter Andrews, 272H, who said he entered the alley at 12.20 am and saw nothing to rouse his suspicions that anything was wrong. At about 12.25 am Sarah Smith, who was deputy of the Whitechapel Baths and Washhouse situated in Castle Alley, retired to bed. Before she did she closed the window of her room that overlooked the entire alley and saw nothing unusual. At about 12.45 am it began to rain. Five minutes later, Constable Andrews returned to the alley as part of his beat, his journey had taken him about twenty-seven minutes. Lying on the pavement on the western side of the alley, he discovered the body of a woman, her head positioned toward the kerb and her feet towards the wall. Andrews noticed that blood was flowing from two stab wound in the left side of her neck and that her skirts had been pulled up, revealing blood on her abdomen, which had been mutilated. The pavement beneath the body was still dry, so her death must have occurred between 12.25 am and 12.45 am, when it started raining.

Andrews blew his police whistle to summon assistance and this attracted the attention of Sarah Smith, who later said she had heard no sound at all from the alley in the twenty-five minutes between closing the window and PC Andrews blowing his whistle. While he was waiting by the body, Andrews heard someone enter the alley and this turned out to be Isaac Jacobs, a local resident, who was on his way to get something to eat. Andrews told Jacobs to stay with the body while he went to get assistance. As he was about to do so Sergeant Edward Badham arrived on the scene after being summoned by Andrews' whistle. Badham had been on duty inspecting the local beat officers in the area and had only recently spoken to Andrews.

At 1.10 am, Inspector Edmund Reid of H Division arrived on the scene, followed a few minutes later by Dr Phillips. Inspector Reid said at the later inquest that he held a 'watching brief' as he believed some coins that were reported to have been found under the body were similar to those in the case of Annie Chapman. The coin found was a bronze farthing which led to the belief that the deception suspected of having been foisted on Annie Chapman – i.e. offering a polished farthing as a sovereign or a sixpence – had been practised on Alice McKenzie as well.

Dr Phillips performed the post-mortem on the body, which was identified as that of Alice McKenzie. The main cause of death was given as severance of the left carotid artery; there were also two stabs in the left side of the neck 'carried forward in the same skin wound', some bruising on the chest, five bruises or marks on the left side of the abdomen, a seven-inch wound 'but not unduly deep' from the bottom of the left breast to the navel, seven or eight scratches beginning at the navel and pointing toward the genitalia and a small cut across the *mons veneris*. Phillips believed that a degree of anatomical knowledge must have been necessary to commit the wounds on Alice's body, but he did not believe that it was the work of the Ripper, noting:

> After careful and long deliberation, I cannot satisfy myself, on purely Anatomical and professional grounds that the perpetrator of all the 'Wh Ch. Murders' is our man. I am on the contrary impelled to a contrary conclusion in this noting the mode of procedure and the character of the mutilations and judging of motive in connection with the latter.
>
> I do not here enter into the comparison of the cases neither do I take into account what I admit may be almost conclusive evidence in favour of the one man theory if all the surrounding circumstances and other evidence are considered, holding it as my duty to report on the P.M. appearances and express an opinion only on Professional grounds, based upon my observation.

Dr Bond, on the insistence of Robert Anderson, examined the body the day after the post-mortem and his report contradicted that of Phillips:

> I see in this murder evidence of similar design to the former Whitechapel murders, viz. sudden onslaught on the prostrate woman, the throat skilfully and resolutely cut with subsequent mutilation, each mutilation indicating sexual thoughts and a desire to mutilate the abdomen and sexual organs. I am of opinion that the murder was performed by the same person who committed the former series of Whitechapel murders.

Anderson, who was on leave at the time of the murder, disagreed with Bond's findings, saying:

I am here assuming that the murder of Alice M'Kenzie on the 17th of July 1889, was by another hand. I was absent from London when it occurred, but the Chief Commissioner investigated the case on the spot and decided it was an ordinary murder, and not the work of a sexual maniac.

James Monro, who was in charge whilst Anderson was away, disagreed: 'I need not say that every effort will be made by the police to discover the murderer, who, I am inclined to believe, is identical with the notorious Jack the Ripper of last year.'

The inquest came to the conclusion that Alice McKenzie's death was caused by the all too familiar 'murder by a person or persons unknown'.

POSTSCRIPT

On 14 January 1891, at the Oakhampton Petty sessions in Devon, James Endacott and his brother Bowden Endacott were summoned, at the insistence of the Oakhampton Board of Guardians, for neglecting to contribute towards the maintenance of their father. The father had become chargeable to the common fund of the Oakhampton Union.

James, a farmer of Mamhead, near Dawlish, had written to the relieving officer of the court and offered to pay 1/6d (7½p) per week, the amount demanded of him by the Guardians.

The relieving officer of the court found out that Bowden Endacott was claiming to be an inspector of police who lived in Tottenham Court Road and had seventeen lodgers. Mr Metherall, the relieving officer, stated that despite writing two letters to Endacott, he had received no reply. It was also stated that Bowden Endacott was the officer involved in the case of Miss Cass.

The court order that Bowden Endacott pay 1/- (5p) a week towards the upkeep of his father. Whether he did or not is not known.

This just goes to show what sort of fantasy world Bowden was living in. He was never an inspector, staying a constable throughout his career, and never lived in Tottenham Court Road.

Bowden Endacott's wife, Emily died on 2 October 1898 of phthisis. He continued serving with the Metropolitan Police until his retirement on 3 September 1900, still on guard duty at the British Museum and still a constable, having never been promoted through the whole of his career. Upon his retirement he moved to Larkbeare Farm in Minehead where he died only five years later on 5 October 1905 of tubercular laryngitis and exhaustion, aged 54. He took his secret to the grave.

Bibliography

Books

Dr Robert Anderson, *The Lighter Side of My Official Life*, extracted and reproduced in *Blackwood's Magazine*, 1910
Paul Begg, Martin Fido, Keith Skinner, *The Jack the Ripper A-Z*, Headline Books, 1996, pp. 57-62
Walter Dew, *I Caught Crippen*, Blackie & Son, 1938
William Booth, *In Darkest England*, The Salvation Army, 1881
Thomas Henry Huxley, *Evolution and Ethics*, Oxford University Press, 1893

Newspapers, Magazines and Reports

East End News
Evening Post, The
The Globe
Hansard
Illustrated Police News
Lancet, The
Lloyd's Weekly Newspaper
London Evening Standard
Manchester Guardian
Mid Sussex Times
Morning Post, The
Murray's Magazine
Pall Mall Gazette
Penny Illustrated Paper
Police Review and Parade Gossip
Reynold's News
Staffordshire Chronicle
Star, The
St James's Gazette
Times, The
Wakefield Free Press
Weekly Herald, The

Organisations

The Devon Constabulary
The Metropolitan Police
The National Archives

Index

Abrahams, F.M, 18, 31
Anderson, Dr Robert, 7, 62–3, 114, 120, 122–3, 125–6
Angel Alley, 46

Barnaby, 5, 112
  See also Burgho
Bartrum, Mr, 18, 31
Blackmail (ing), 20, 28–9, 61, 91
Bond, Dr Thomas, 7, 110, 112–4, 117, 120, 125
Bowman, Mrs, 15–8, 20–3, 25–7, 32–3, 35–7, 39–40
Britannia, The, 68–70, 108, 111
British Museum, The, 10, 15, 35, 44, 102, 126
Buck's Row. 6, 47, 53–56, 58, 84, 115
Burgho, 5, 112
  See also Barnaby

Cass, Elizabeth, 9, 11, 13–44, 102, 126
  See also Langley
Chagford, 8
Chamberlain, Joseph, 17–8
Chapman, Annie, 2, 6, 65, 67–78, 107, 123, 125
Cooney's Lodging House, 92
Crossinghams Lodging House, 46–7, 63, 68–70, 74, 107
  See also Donovan, Timothy: Evans, John

Devon Constabulary, 9–10, 24
Dew, Chief Inspector, Walter, 89
Donovan, Timothy, 68–70

Eddowes, Catherine, 2, 6–7, 79, 82, 87, 91–104, 121
Endacott, Bowden, 2, 8, 10–1, 13–44, 54, 59, 76–7, 91, 94, 96–7, 101–3, 116, 120, 126
Estill, Brian T, 10
Evans, John, 70

Flower and Dean Street, 51–2, 65, 80, 92, 94, 107, 109, 120. 124

George Yard, 6, 46, 120
Gower Street, 10, 79, 102
Grantham, 21, 38

Hanbury Street, 6, 53–5, 58, 61, 65, 71–2, 77, 84, 115, 123

Kelly, Mary Jane, 2, 5–7, 105–19, 121
Kidney, Michael, 79–80, 82

Langley, 23, 37, 39, 44
Leather Apron, 61, 63–66, 68, 73, 80
  See also Pizer, John
Leman Street, 5–6, 65, 80, 82

Llewellyn, Dr Rees, Ralph, 55–7

Matthews, Henry, 4–5, 17–19
McKenzie, Alice, 120, 123, 125
Millwood, Annie, 119
Mizen, P.C. Jonas, 53–5, 58
Monro, James, 4–5, 29, 126
Mulshaw, Patrick, 55–56
Mylett, Rose, 120, 123

Neil, P.C. John, 54–56
Newton, Mr, 16–7
Nichols, Mary Ann, 2, 45, 49–61

Oxford Circus, 14–5, 25, 32
Oxford Street, 13, 23, 32, 35, 37, 40

Pietra, Fernande, 27–8
Pizer, John, 63–66, 68
Prostitute (s), 2–3, 6, 8, 14–5, 17, 19–20, 24–6, 28–9, 34, 44–7, 49–51, 53, 61, 63, 69, 72, 79, 91, 105–9, 119–20, 123

Regent Street, 14–9, 21–2, 25, 27–8, 32, 35, 37, 41, 43
Reid, Inspector, Edmund, 124

Southampton Row, 15, 19, 36
Stockton, 21, 23–4, 34, 37–9
Stride, Elizabeth, 2, 6, 79–90, 121

Tabram, Martha, 6, 45–8, 119–20
Ten Bells, The, 70, 108
Thain, P.C. John, 53–6
Thick, Sergeant, William, 64–5

Vaughan, Mr, 31–3

Warren, Sir Charles, 4–5, 13–4, 17–20, 23–5, 27–8, 88, 96–7
Wheatley, James, 25–6
Wilson, Ada, 120